SWEETWATER SAILORS - THE REST OF THE STORY

SWEETWATER SAILORS - THE REST OF THE STORY

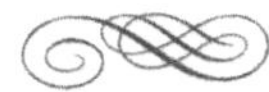

BOB OJALA

A3Pi Services, LLC

Contents

SWEETWATER SAILORS –
The Rest of the Story

The families, unusual sailors, and people not typically remembered, who work in Great Lakes Maritime Industries.

Bob Ojala

ISBN: 978-1-0880-8015-3

DEDICATION

To my father, Matt Ojala, who sailed the Great Lakes for 32 years.

In 2020, I published Sweetwater Sailors. It was (and remains) very popular amongst Great Lakes "Boat Nerds," and was also my first attempt at collaborating with sailors to share the everyday lives of Great Lakes Merchant Mainers. However, when it came to gathering stories for that first book, it was a little challenging since many sailors' wives were reluctant to participate. I am happy to say that after the release and moderate success of Sweetwater Sailors, many who were initially hesitant, came to view this as a serious project and were ready to submit stories for this sequel. This book is now THE REST OF THE STORY!

I owe a huge debt of gratitude to some experienced Great Lakes sailors, who contributed stories and photographs for this book. In particular, numerous wives offered much time and wrote many working drafts of their stories contained herein. I'm sure my contributors became frustrated with my constant reminders to send me their stories, but I hope they are proud of what we have created here.

I've worked aboard these ships, but did not have much actual sailing experience, so, with the help of these men and women, this book has become what I believe to be a true representation of what life is like aboard the ships, ferries, passenger boats, tugs and marine construction equipment which operate on the Great Lakes.

This book also describes the understanding, dedication, and "get-er-done" attitudes of those wives who stay at home, raise the children, pay the bills, repair the house, shovel the snow, and do their best to have a social life, as if they were a single-parent, while their partners work for months aboard ship. And when the sailor comes home.........well, I'll let you read about it!

I

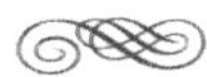

INTRODUCTION

For readers who have read *Sweetwater Sailors*, this sequel is quite different from the first book. None of the stories are repeated, and only a few of the original sailors who contributed stories, appear again in this book.

I believe *Sweetwater Sailors* had a very good representation of women who sailed the Great Lakes, including two women captains, one of whom is still the only woman captain on a U.S. flagged, Great Lakes ore carrier, and also three women Chief Engineers.

In this book, you will find even more stories of women of various capacities within the Great Lakes Marine industry. I have stories from some women chefs (they are too talented to be called cooks), and from some Canadian sailors, who were not included in the previous book (though not on purpose). I've also had a very positive response from the sailors' wives, to this second book, and I am very pleased with their contributions. These are the women (and I'm sure some men as well) who stay at home while their sailor/partner is gone for months at a time. Without the support and understanding of their partners, many sailors' lives would be very stressed. So, don't just appreciate the contributions of our dedicated sailors, but also give a lot of credit to their spouses or partners, who put up with the hardships of taking care of life at home, making decisions alone, and then trying to change priorities each time the sailor comes home during their time off the ship. Based on the experience of my own parents, IT AIN'T EASY!

How to Read this Book: The stories included in this book are mostly told in the first-person by each author/contributor. In some chapters, I inject my thoughts and contributions to the stories, using italics, so that each contributor's story stands out from my voice. There are areas where I introduce contributors and their stories with some background information or narrate their stories as they were told to me (using italics). There are also areas where I share my experiences within another contributor's story. Those thoughts are also shared using italics.

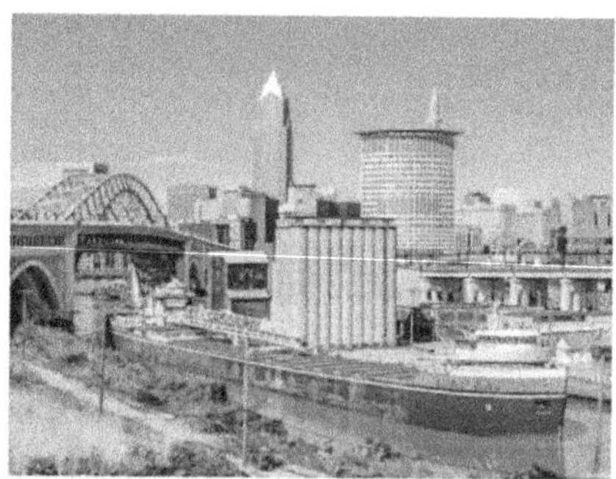

The picture above might look a little scary to those who are not familiar with the navigation skills required to enter Great Lakes ports, but these ships do this several times each week (*Wilfred Sykes* entering Cleveland's Cuyahoga River). Now, I'm familiar with the

Great Lakes, but the picture below is the one that represents pure terror, in my eyes. The same river, by the way!

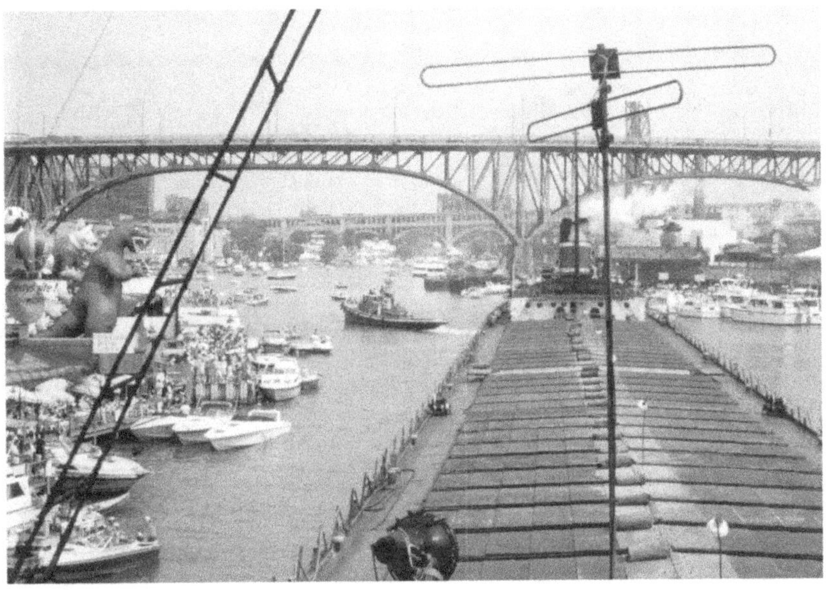

2

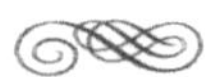

WOMEN WHO SAIL THE GREAT LAKES

I have been asked many times why someone would want to become a sailor, especially after I've just told them that a sailor's life is difficult, even dangerous, and tough on their families. The truth is that while being a sailor is not always the exciting, even romantic, life that the general public pictures it to be, it can still be a rewarding and fulfilling career for those who commit to it. As you will see in the pages that follow, many women have sacrificed and committed to the life of either having a career as a sailor or being married to one. Each woman has an unusual story to share.

I'm starting this section on Women Sailors on the Great Lakes with Sabrina Wiater's story because her explanation of her 'WHY' is excellent and should be read by any young person, not just a woman, who is considering a career in the maritime industry.

For minor clarification, Sabrina's father managed a fleet of ore carriers on the Great Lakes after going ashore. He was also a captain.

The following story is written by Sabrina, word for word.

3

SABRINA WIATER

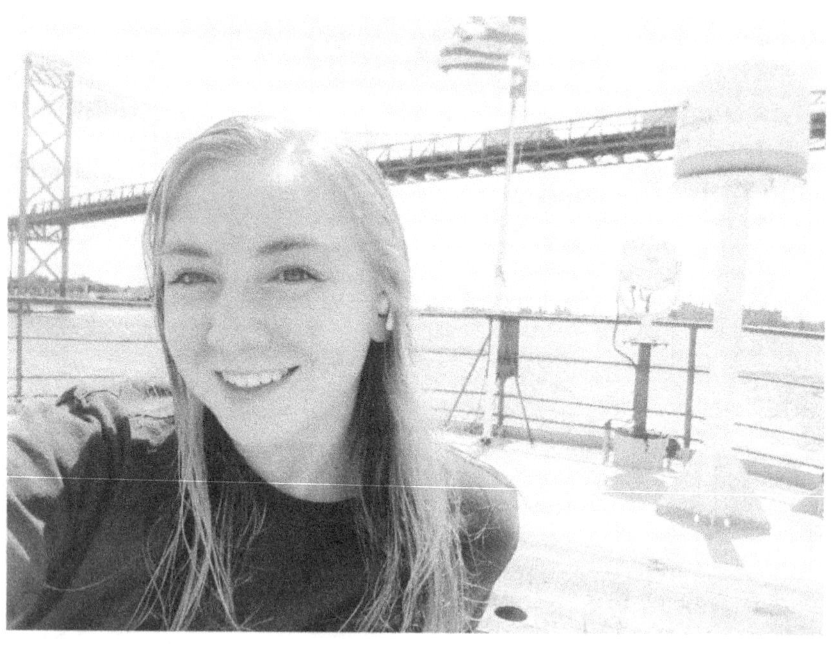

High school happens to be a pretty good place to start. Especially in 11th grade when I was dual enrolled in the local, state university satellite school to pursue a degree in chemistry. As it turns out, I did not like chemistry, and it certainly did not like me. I was pretty much back at square one with what I wanted to do with my life, a question to this day I'm not sure why we are asking 16-year-olds to answer.

I always knew about the maritime industry, in theory, but for the most part, it was just my dad's job. I knew that he used to sail, but ever since I can remember, he worked an average 9-5 office job with an above-average stress level and a phone that never stopped ringing. He had brought me along to the boats every once in a while, but it wasn't like I had some sort of inside knowledge of what the big picture was, why everything was happening, what the boats were there to do, and how it shaped our lives. I think this kind of limbo was really what prompted my decision to go to the Maritime Academy. It was comfortable enough that I somewhat knew the industry, but still mysterious enough to be an exciting choice.

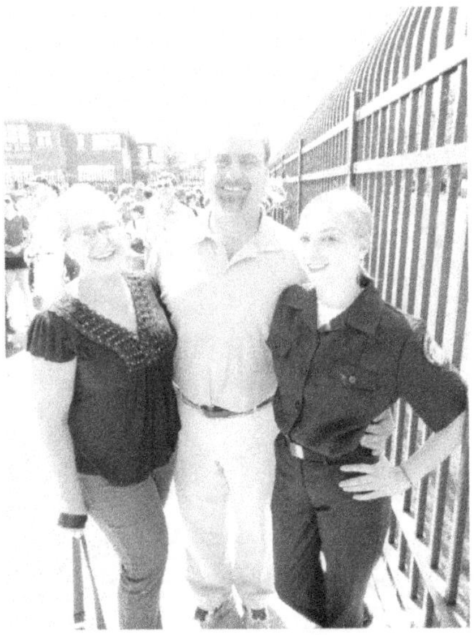

My mom and dad dropping me off on my
first day of "Pre-Fall", and of course, I was
the only cadet to forget their name tag

Once you decide to apply, your next big choice is to decide if you are going to pursue the deck department or the engine department. Even though he is a Captain, my dad had never shied away from saying that engineering was the much more practical way to go. I didn't understand why at the time, but I did take his advice and applied to the engineering department. If you ask him now, he will tell you that he was having trouble finding a promising new Chief Engineer, *so he was going to just build his own.*

"I think everyone likes to say they are mechanically inclined, but truth be told, the extent of my mechanical ability pretty much began and ended at holding the flashlight while my dad told me to let him know when I saw TDC on the tractor engine. This kept me up at night, as I was worried that I would already be behind my other classmates before the year even began. I tried to push that feeling away and remind myself that the whole purpose of college was to teach.

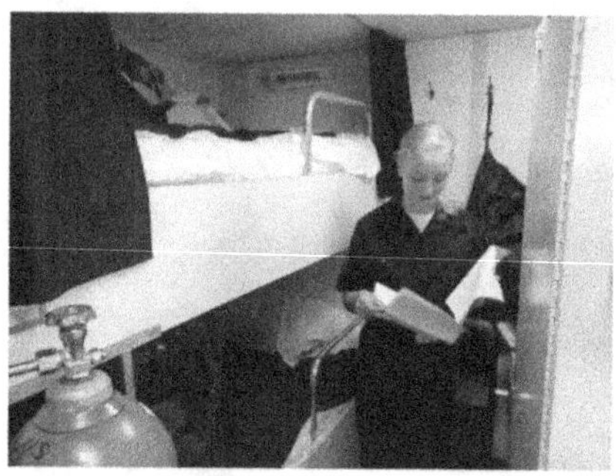

Over these two weeks, you are taking two courses: Survival at Sea and Introduction to Marine Engineering. My first "notable" experience happened in the Survival at Sea course. The class is exactly how it sounds, emergency training in case things go wrong while underway. You learn how to fire flares, don a survival suit, and row a lifeboat. The lifeboat is typically directed by a coxswain. At the end of the course, the instructors assign you certain roles and you are tested and graded on your skills. I ended up being assigned as coxswain of the lifeboat. I was not very confident in the role, and I ended up steering the lifeboat right into the side of the training ship, in front of 60 of my peers. To say it was mortifying was probably an understatement.

When the second class was over, I headed straight to my car, still packed to the brim with everything I owned for college, and sat there. 'You can just leave,' I told myself, 'you can just drive home right now.' Every feeling of inadequacy that I had spent the summer squashing down had somehow unfolded in the front seat of my o1 Nissan Pathfinder. I still don't know what made me get out of the car and go back to the training ship, but I did.

we are all in this together and we are all going to make it to the finish line! who is and isn't good enough to be here O h you better have a thick skin if you're going to make it in this industry,' T his isn't for the faint of heart; you better be ready to be put through your paces out there if I had only known then, what I know now.

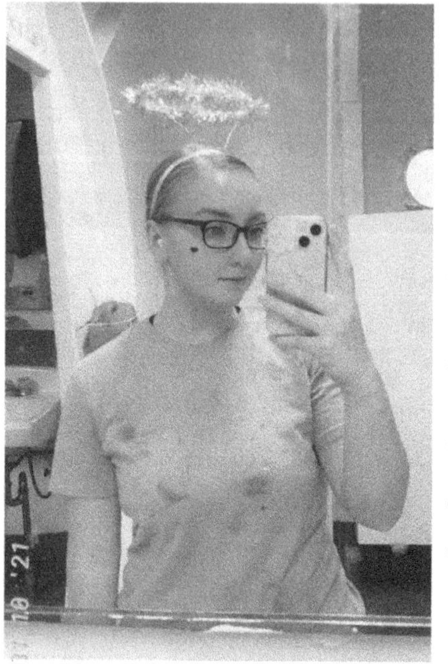

I ended up getting stuck on the boat for all of the fall holidays this last year, including Halloween, which was my favorite. I'm never going to miss an opportunity to put on an angel halo and spray myself with glitter. My co-workers and I had a good laugh about it, and no one thought any less of me. The galley was decorated to spooky nines, and we even carved pumpkins.

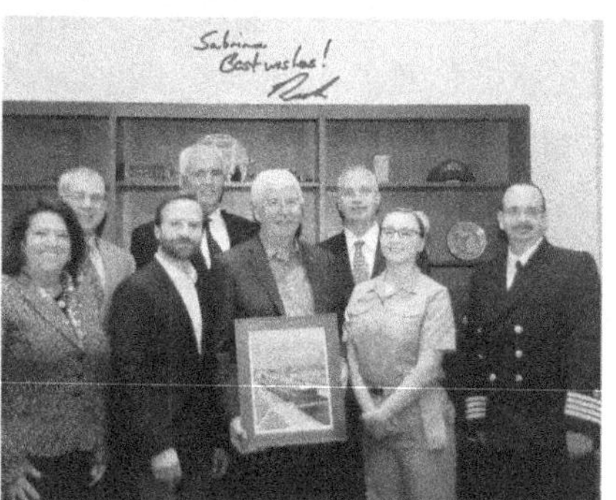

In this picture: I got to meet former Governor Rick Snyder when he allocated part of Michigan's budget to the plan by the Army Corps of Engineers to build a new Soo Lock. Also pictured are Jim Weakly from Lake Carriers Association, Captain Mike Surgalski from GLMA, and Mark Barker from Interlake, among others.

I was so worried about how I was going to fare in the industry because of what my classmates had told me. But truth be told, all the guys who made those remarks were 18 years old and fresh out of high school. They had never been on a ship before. They had no insight into 'what the industry was really like,' or some secret knowledge. Yeah, maybe they had heard some horror stories from their grandpa who sailed during WWII, but the truth is, that mindset in shipping is almost 100 years old. The best part about the guys who gave me the most trouble – they ended up dropping out, flunking out, or getting kicked out.

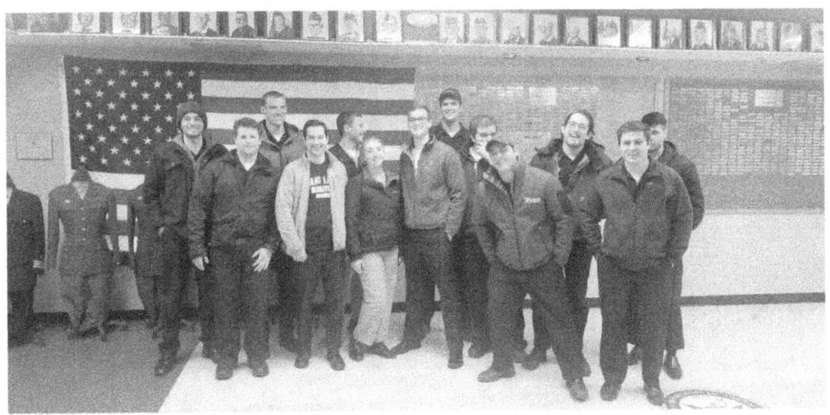

The remainder of the GLMA Engine Class of 2020 who finished
the program and successfully wrote their USCG license.

While the shipping industry is typically behind the curve compared to shoreside, and maybe it's a little rough around the edges at times, a lot of that is due to the average age of the mariners. The older the working generation, the older the mindset is. But it turned out not nearly this terrifying environment that it was painted to be. For the most part, it's a pretty regular job. You might get into the occasional riff with a coworker, but that happens at shoreside jobs too. The pressure can be a little bit higher because you eat and live in the same place, but because of that, people genuinely try to keep the peace among themselves.

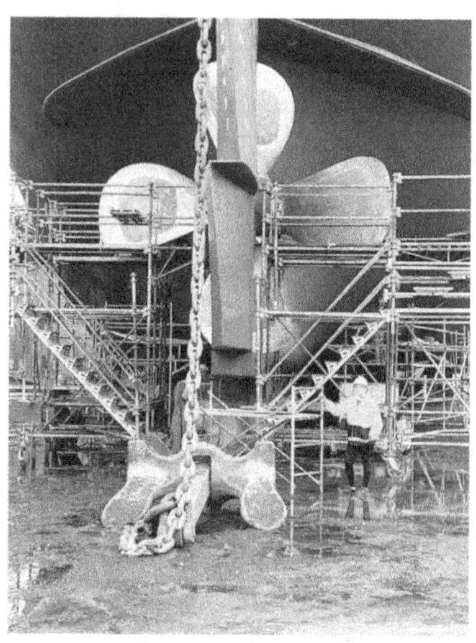

Of course, there are diffi-cult aspects to the job; it's very demanding mentally, physically, and emotionally. It's long hours, it's hard work, and realizing that life is continuing back at home without you, takes a huge toll on you. Because of that, I try to stick to my 60 on, 30 off rotation. I want to go home and spend time

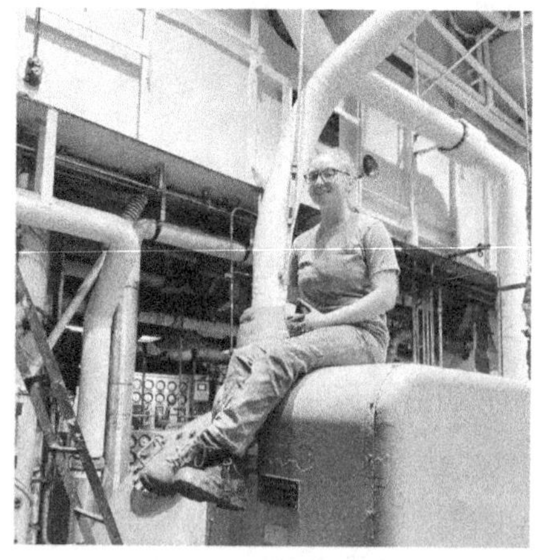

with my family, and I want to enjoy my hobbies. I hear stories of people staying out for more than 120 days, and that's just not for me. But that's kind of what is nice about the industry, you have the option to choose how much or how little you would like to work.

This is a good place to talk about that ever-present question: '*What are you going to do when you have kids?*' I always see this as an inappropriate question, in any scenario, but it's still the number one thing I get asked. And the answer is – I have no idea. Any parent will tell you that if you have a 'plan' for when you will, or should, have children, just go ahead, and throw it in the trash. Children are such a life-altering occurrence that there is no way to predict how you will react. Tons of people leave their regular 9-5 lives to stay home.

Tons of mariners leave the industry to see their children every day. For example, my father left sailing to watch me grow up, and that never made him less of a person to do so. But because I am '*mom,*' it's automatically assumed that I will just stop sailing, and it's never a noble thing the way it is for a man. It insinuates that I'm not dedicated to the job, or that I'm not a permanent part of the crew, and this is just a casual phase in my life. And that very well may be the case. I may have children and decide to come home. Or I may decide to continue sailing and just scale back the number of days that I am gone, the same way plenty of fathers do. This decision does not make them any less of a good parent. Either way, it is absolutely none of their goddamn business. That is a decision that will be made by me and my husband when the time comes. I don't need to have an answer now, because now I am here, and now I am a permanent part of the crew.

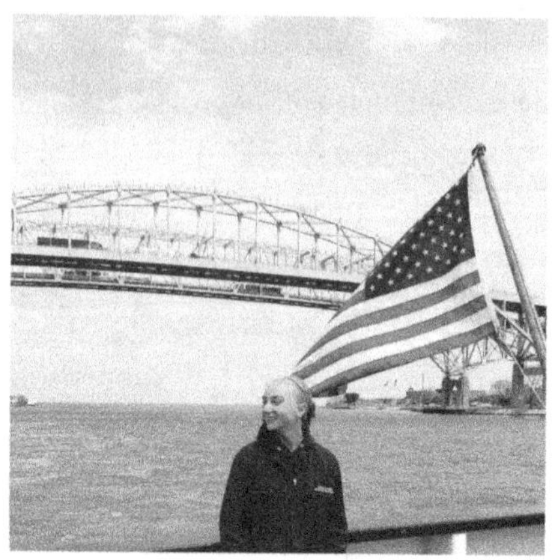

On my very first job out of college, I sailed as the Junior Third Engineer on the *Philip R. Clarke*, with Kate Walheim as the First. Not only was it just really an inspiration to see a woman in a higher role in my department on a ship, but she ended up saving my ass once (literally). Another engineer and I were trying to lift a heavy motor, and I had bent at the knees to save my back. In doing this, I ended up splitting my coveralls wide open. I'm talking a good 12-14in split right on my butt. I was wearing underwear, but I felt like they almost made the situation worse. I'm in the very belly of the ship, in the lowermost level of the engine room, and I have no idea how I am going to get back to my stateroom without exposing myself to my coworkers. I called down for Kate and she was able to cover me long enough so that I could get to a rag bin and find a large enough piece of cloth to patch up the tear and get me out of the engine room with my dignity intact.

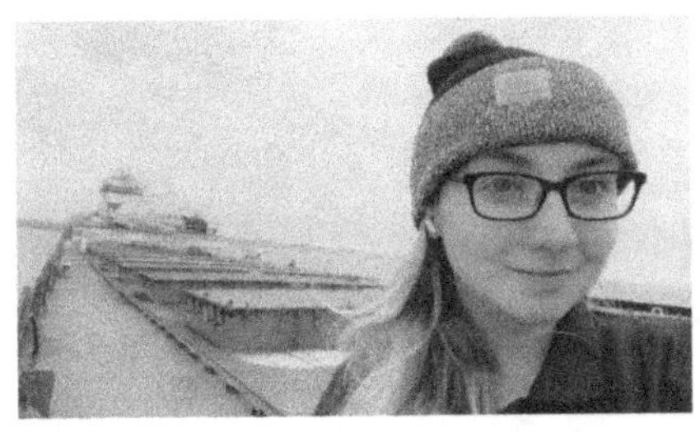

Currently, I am sailing as the permanent Third Assistant Engineer aboard the SS *Wilfred Sykes*. I am extremely lucky to be able to say that I love my job, and a lot of it is because of the crew. I have a great Chief Engineer who has always been there to speak out when I didn't feel confident enough to speak up for myself. I've also had other Assistant Engineers who were more concerned with 'nipping anything inappropriate' in the bud than they were at keeping the peace. I have a deck department that has always treated me with kindness and respect. I have a Captain who told me "Welcome Home" when I signed on for a hitch. I know that it's not always the case, and I know some other women have much harder experiences, but I hope that those interested in the industry know that these experiences are out there, and they should not stop until they find what best suits them.

I noticed an uptick in women applying during my time at GLMA, and I've sailed with them in passing during my career. I really hope that this penny for my thoughts brings a young woman, interested in the maritime industry, some comfort in knowing that she has a place out here and that she is welcome.

4

ALEXANDRIA BARRETT

Sabrina's story addressed the issue of family, and whether or not to continue sailing when and if one decides to have a family. I think Alexandria's story is a good follow-up to Sabrina's because Alexandria quit sailing and has used her Marine Engineering experience as an asset in her shore job.

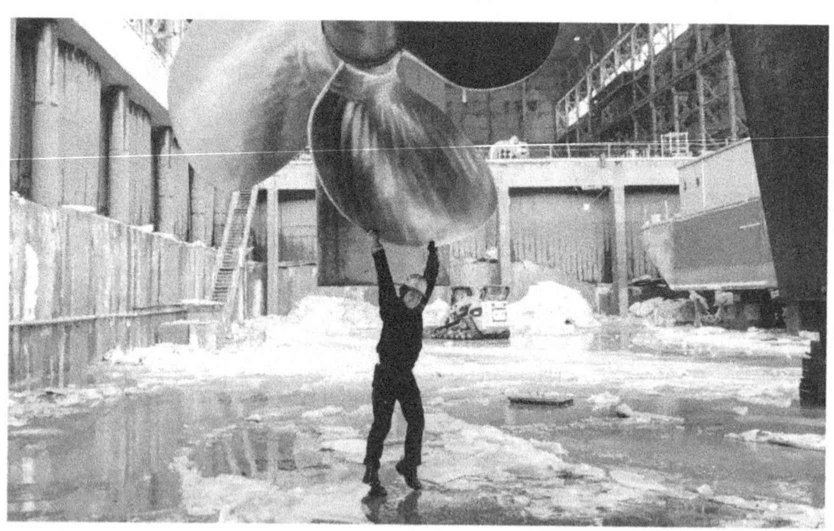

My name is Alexandria Barrett, some know me as 'Lexi'. When I was 19, I decided to attend the Great Lakes Maritime Academy and become a sailor. I come from a long line of engineers. Whether white-collar or blue-collar, engineering has always been in my DNA, so I decided to become an engineer, not a captain!

The combination of being both a sailor and engineer seemed like the perfect combination!

I feel it is important to discuss where you come from, so I was born in Flint, Michigan, and spent my younger years in a farm town outside Flint. My love for the water started at a young age as I grew up like any Michigander spending my weekends 'up north' at my Great Grandparent's cabin on Lake Huron. As time passed and my family and I moved to Northern California, just outside of Napa Valley, I would often spend as much time as I could at Stinson Beach, Bodega Bay, and Point Reyes Seashore. I vividly remember watching the freighters pass and daydreaming about being out to sea. My interest peaked in maritime after visiting California Maritime during my sophomore year.

As life continued to shift, I found myself back in Michigan working at Mott Community College in Flint, when I was 18 years old. I was then able to gain admission to Great Lakes Maritime through a connection between the Motts director and the former admissions director of Great Lakes Maritime Academy, John Berck. I loved the academy and Traverse City. I finally got my wish to sail on the West Coast as a cadet. I spent my time on the *M/V Manoa*, which did the 'Pineapple Run' from Oakland, California, to Honolulu, Hawaii, Seattle, Washington, and Oakland. I did that for five months.

Only a True Michigander...I once had someone tell me that only a true Michigander can go to Great Lakes Maritime Academy, work on a freighter and complete their master's from Kettering

University (formerly General Motors Institute GMI) while out to sea on the Great Lakes. I often take great pride in that comment.

Only a True Michigander...I once had someone tell me that only a true Michigander can go to Great Lakes Maritime Academy, work on a freighter and complete their master's from Kettering University (formerly General Motors Institute GMI) while out to sea on the Great Lakes. I often take great pride in that comment.

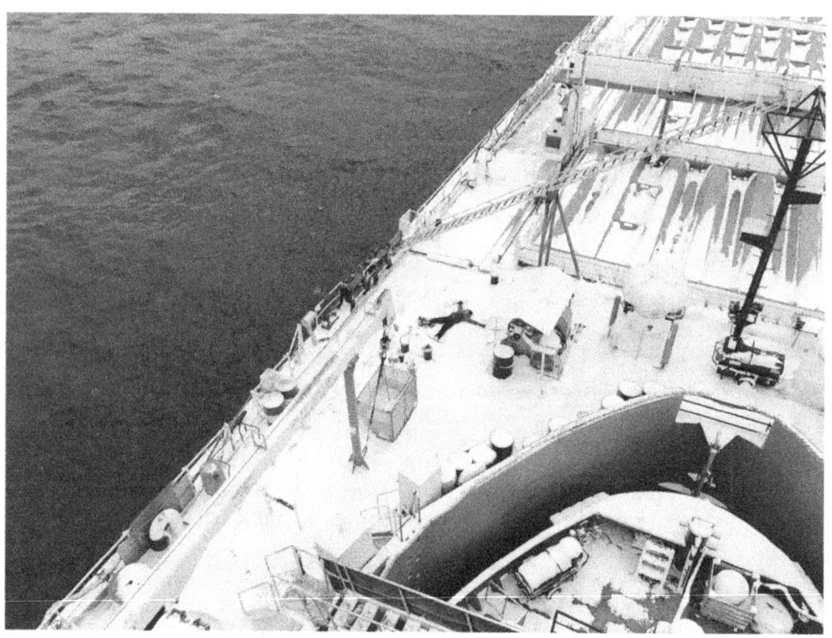

Alexandria making a 'Snow Angel' on the deck.

Erie PA Dry Dock – 2017...One evening, three of us drove thru a blizzard and 'wrangled' the *Olive Moore/Menominee*, a tug-barge, that needed some help.

It all started when I was working Winter Work in 2017, and another lake effect snowstorm rolled through the towns of Lake Erie. I was working on the Articulated Tug Barge (ATB) *Ashtabula/*

Defiance, and we were on shore power, sitting on the blocks for a dry dock inspection.

I had already been at the dry dock for a few weeks, and I must mention that before I arrived for winter work, I had just bought a new 2017 Silverado 1500, 'Special Ops' Edition (because I thought I was special). I picked the truck up in Flint, Michigan, right outside the truck plant. I drove my overpriced blacked-out Silverado around the shipyard with pride.

This evening in question, when the lake effect snow took place, Chief Sonny asked me, the other engineer, Sean Gardiner, and an able-bodied seaman, Dave Tyson, to go to Ashtabula, Ohio, and bring soft lines to another tug/barge, the *Olive Moore/Menominee*. The tug and barge had blown off the dock and broken some soft lines and cables.

We all went onto the barge *Ashtabula* at 2000 hours and loaded up my new 'Special Ops' Silverado with four soft lines in the truck's bed and numerous heaving lines. The Chief knew what he was doing. The three of us loaded up my truck and drove through a blizzard to get to Ashtabula, usually only a 45-minute drive along Lake Erie, but this evening it took us almost two hours.

When we made it to the dock, we had to create a pulley system to get the soft lines up to the men on the barge. The AB, Tyson, threw a soft line up to the guys stuck on the barge, and we created a chain and attached the lines to the ball hitch on my truck. I then drove forward and back, pulling the ship in. At the time, this may sound like a real horror story. However, it turned out to be one of my favorite moments while working in the Great Lakes maritime industry. It defined and solidified my friendship with Dave Tyson and Sean, and secondly, it just went to show how Chevy Trucks are the best trucks ever made.

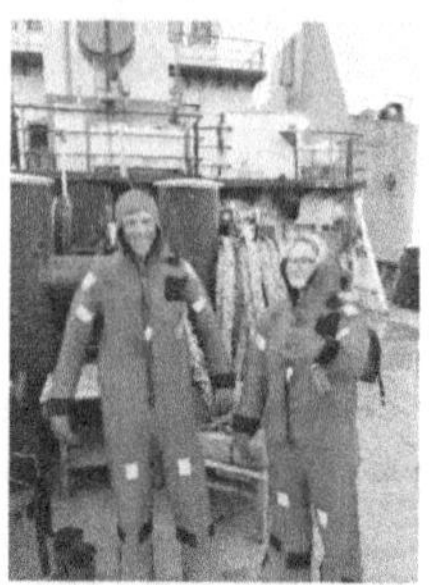

Here I am in this picture with Chief Engineer, Jim "Sonny" Collum.

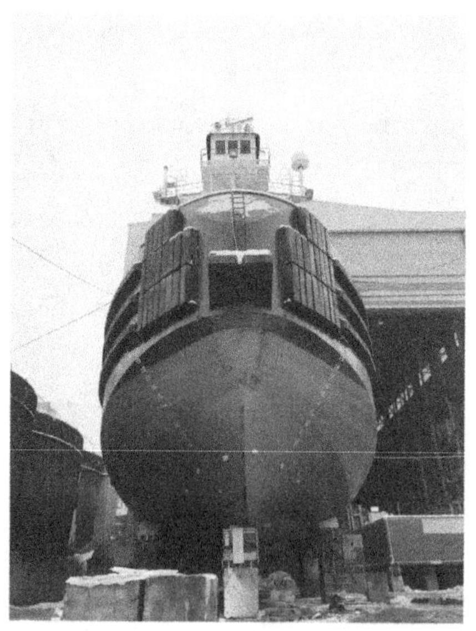

All kidding aside, my time spent in Erie, Pennsylvania, was excellent. I had the opportunity to take the *Ashtabula/Defiance* into dry dock, which only occurs every five years. I got to walk around a vessel in a dry dock with inspectors, engineers, welders, ABS

Surveyors, and the ship's crew. I was humbled by how much I had yet to learn, and it made me excited for all that I would learn.

All 'sea stories' aside, my experience with Grand River Navigation gave me a lot of opportunities. It was my first adult job, and I started as a third engineer working at Sturgeon Bay shipyard on the M/V *Calumet*. One of my first jobs at the shipyard was assisting one of the engineers, Matt Phillips, in installing a valve in a ballast tank. We got right in there, and he took the time to show me how to do it properly - and eventually, I installed ballast valves myself.

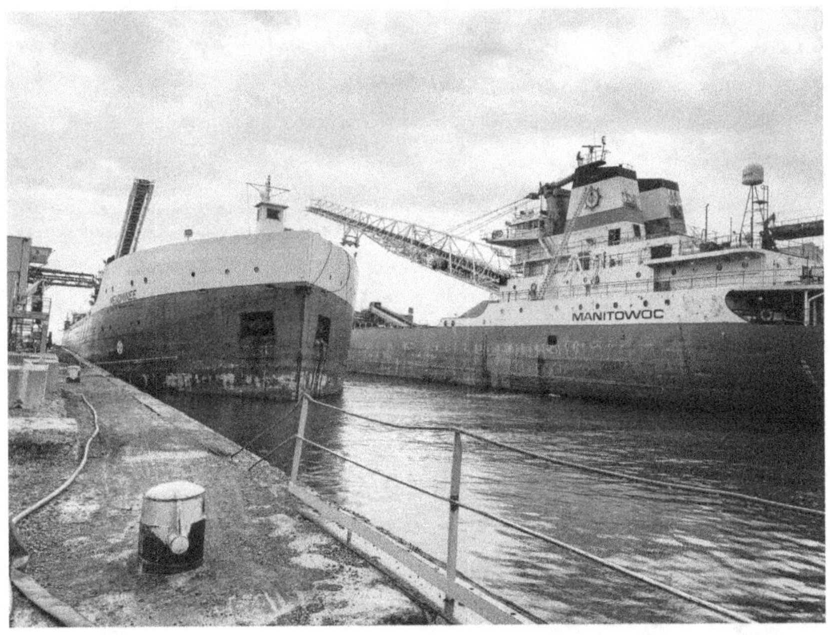

I kept my friendships and relationships with Grand River, and now I am back working for them as a contractor. They were my official first contract! I have made it full circle with the company.

Who says you can't find love at sea? It may be frowned upon to meet your spouse out at sea – but it does happen to the best of us. I met my husband while out to sea on the Great Lakes, and we went on our first date in Rogers City, Michigan. We got off the ship in Calcite and walked up to the legendary sailor's bar, Grekas, and it has been history ever since. I must thank the Chief for letting us go up the street that night since he takes credit for our meeting there.

We now live in New Hampshire and have a beautiful little boy.

My favorite part about sailing...My favorite part about being a sailor would be telling people that I was a sailor. I took great pride in telling people that while working on the Great Lakes. Almost just as much, I loved how people would look at me in disbelief when I told them I was a Great Lakes sailor. *The only other title I love more than being known as a sailor is 'Mom'.*

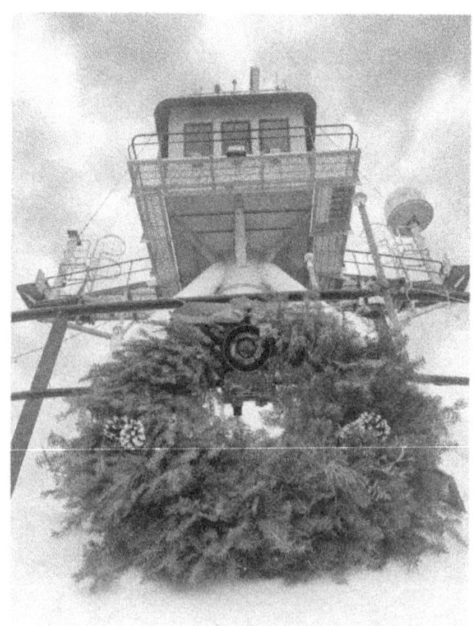

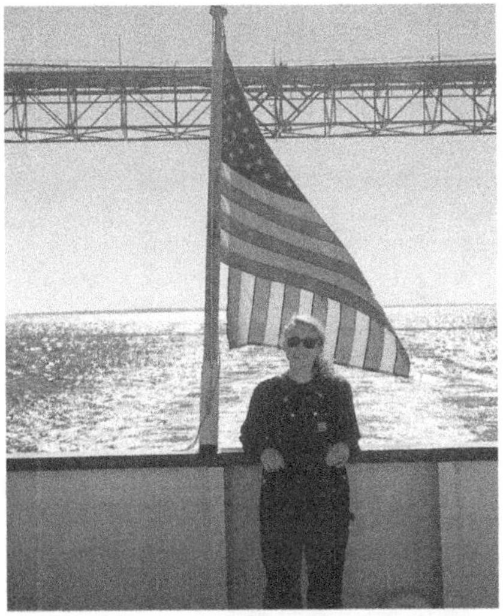

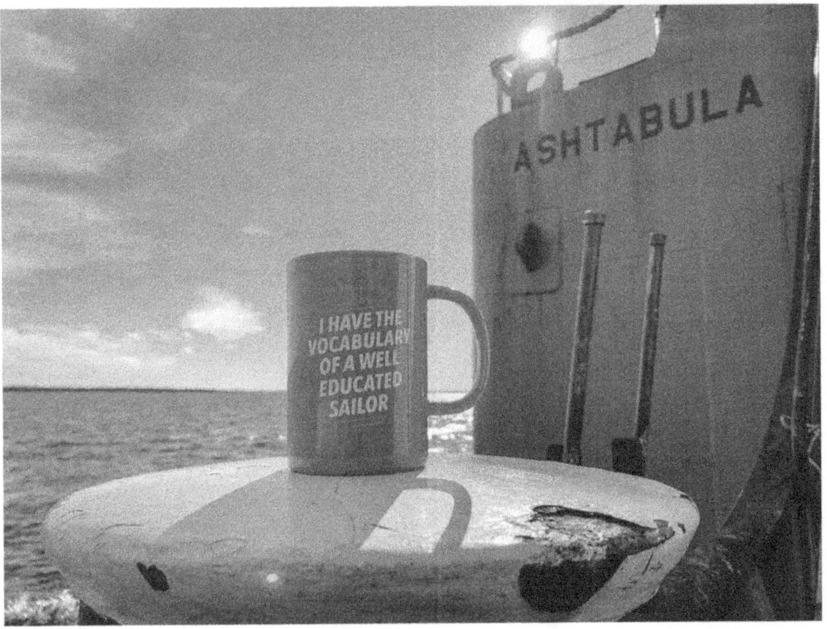

Sailing on the Great Lakes was some of the best years of my life. I made lifelong friends, met the love of my life, and developed a respect for the water, and the sailors out there doing the work. It is an industry that is *almost* romantic. The ups and downs are drastic. You have both a love and hate for what you do. Sea stories are Shakespearean tales that end in tragedy or comedy.

5

WOMEN COOKS ON THE GREAT LAKES

Although women have always sailed the Great Lakes, the numbers have certainly increased in recent years. Early women sailors worked mainly as cooks and stewards because those were the only jobs available for women in those days. Things have certainly changed, and today's cooks on the Great lakes are in a class above, rivaling the chefs at many shoreside restaurants.

I should mention that, in my life, I have always been one to cook a lot. I started cooking when I was a child, during some extended illnesses in my mother's life. I still enjoy cooking and do the majority of the cooking at home these days. I am not a great cook, but I am imaginative, maybe even adventurous.

When I started noticing some posts on Facebook from a group called Cooks of the Great Lakes, I was amazed by the extravagant menu choices I saw, both of those described and those pictured in the posts. While members in Cooks of the Great Lakes include both men and women, the posts that impressed me the most were the ones by the women.

6

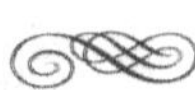

KARI NUSBAUM

One of the women from the *Cooks of the Great Lakes* Facebook group is Kari Nusbaum, who has sailed for Key Lakes Shipping and is now with Interlake. She has been sailing for four years, although she started sailing as a passenger in 2012. Kari lives in Wisconsin when she is not sailing, she has three daughters and seven grandkids, whom she loves with all her heart and misses when she's gone.

I contacted Kari and asked her if she would be willing to contribute some stories to this book, and she said, 'yes'. At first, I thought Kari was Canadian because many of the Cooks on *Cooks of the Great Lakes* are Canadian. Nope! She is a Minnesotan transplanted to Wisconsin!

Before sailing, Kari was the Kitchen Manager for the Minnesota Department of Forestry and fed thousands of firefighters for the Boundary Waters and Ham Lake fires.

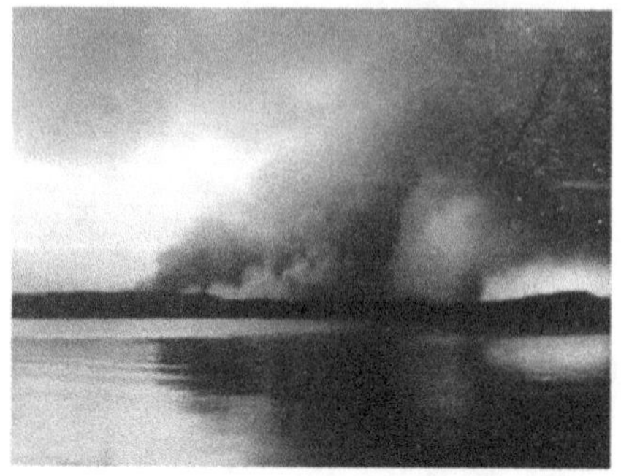

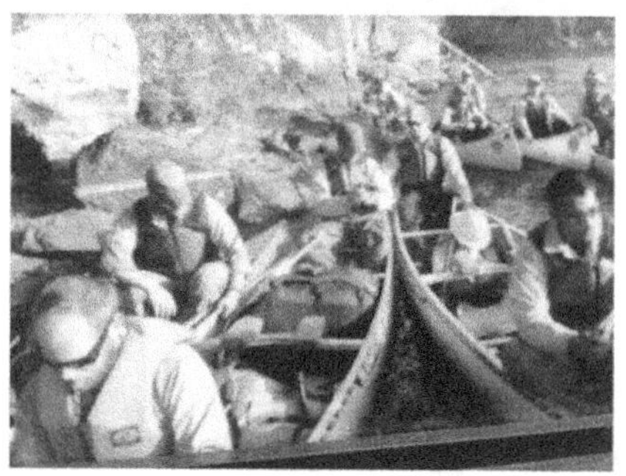

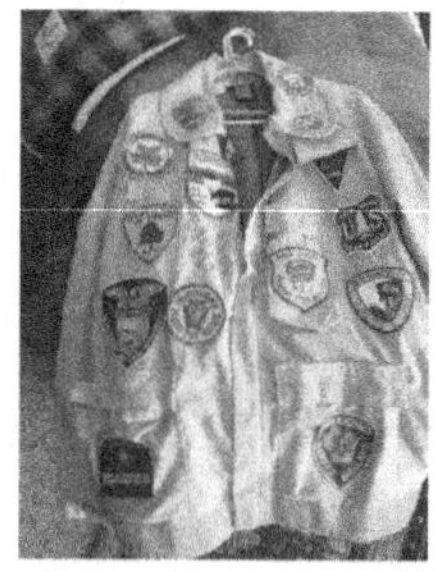

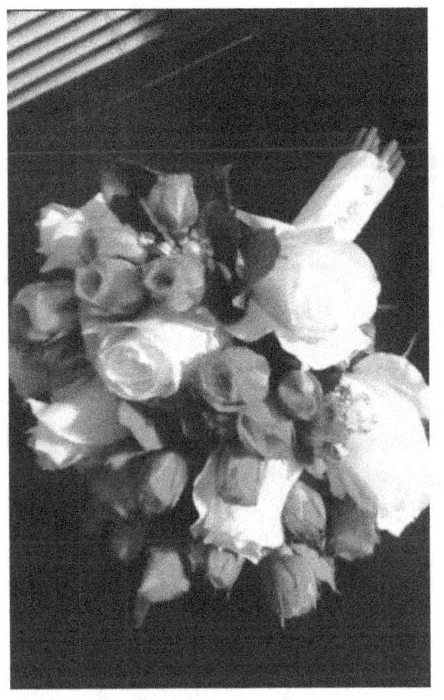

She also owned a wedding services business, which also included decorating cakes and preparing food. In Kari's own words, "I used to own a painting business, doing a faux painting for the big clients. Then I used to be a manager for the floral department at SAMs club. I kept myself busy. I loved being involved with so many things."

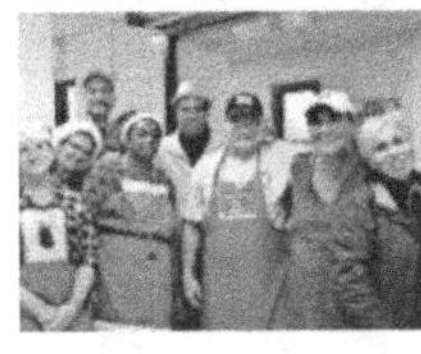

During her off-time, Kari volunteers for a charity, cooking dinners for the homeless.

(I apologize for the poor quality of some of the pictures, but they were too important not to include here.)

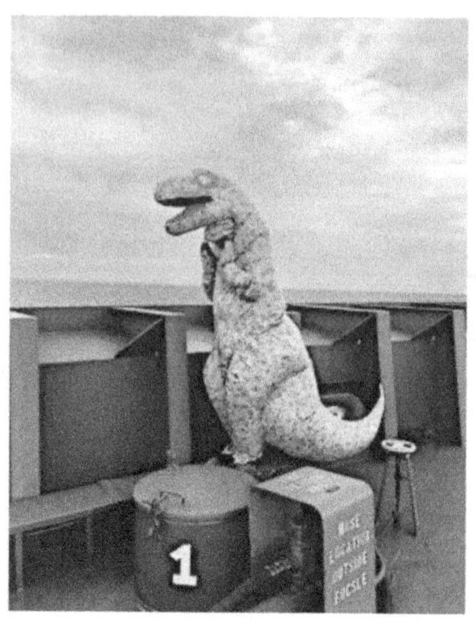

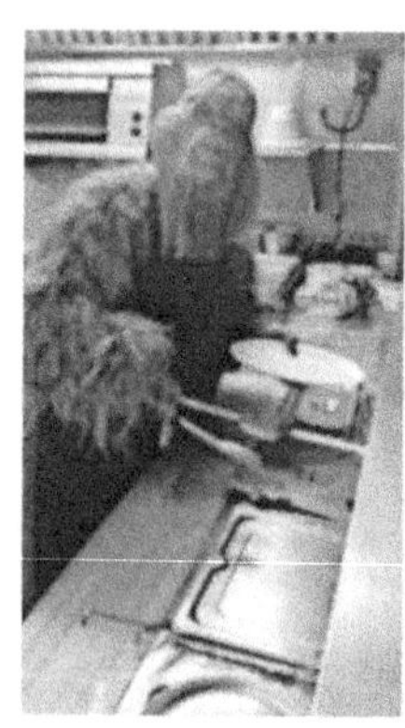

Kari also likes to "spice" up life for the crew by dressing in costume while aboard ship, not to mention her creative cook◆ing. You may notice, I'm a big seafood fan!

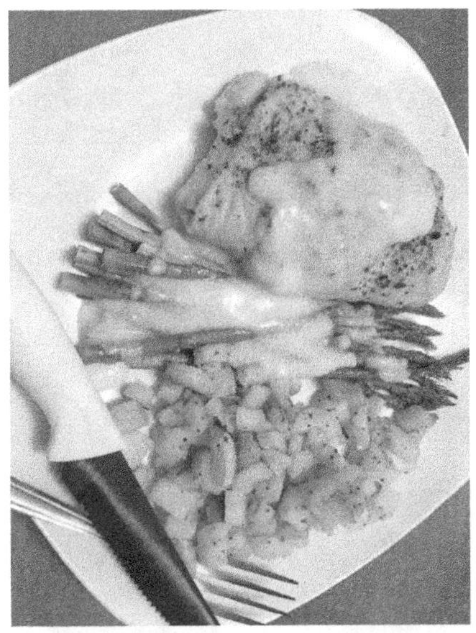

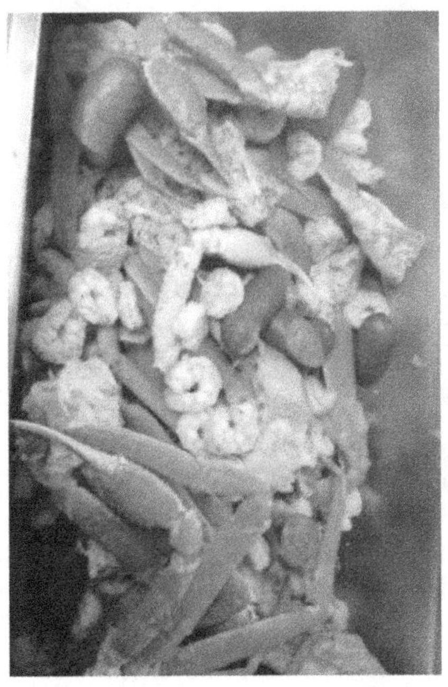

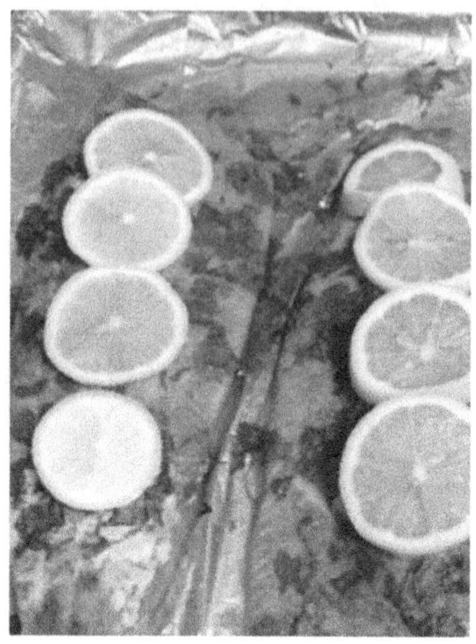

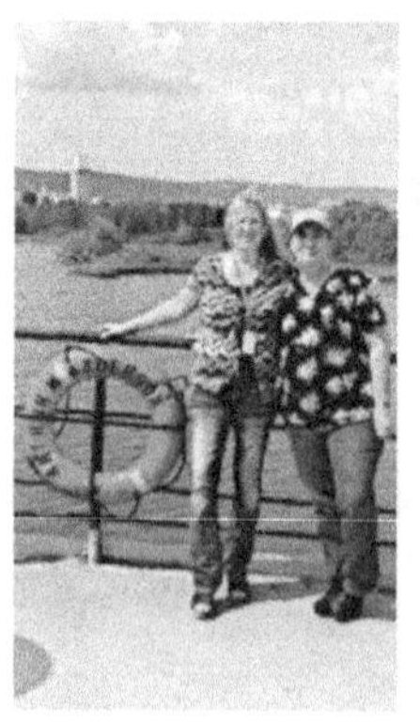

Kari told me she became interested in sailing cargo ships after she rode the Roger Blough with her best friend, Maggie. Kari loved going through the locks and sightseeing, but she got bored and started hanging out in the galley. She even helped with serving food on the Blough.

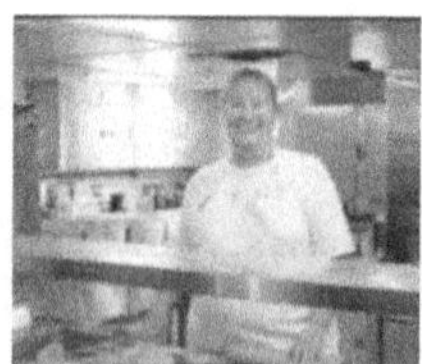

She fell in love with being out on the water but was married at the time. It wasn't until she was separated from her husband that her friend helped her get her first job working with Key Lakes. She stayed with Key Lakes for a few years before moving on and going to work at Interlake. According to Kari, she took the job at Interlake because they offered her more work. She does Relief jobs now but may take a permanent position once she has finished working on her house.

In Kari's words: "It's hard because you can't please everyone out here, and it's really hard for a relief cook because we have to learn the likes and dislikes of everyone in the crew. Sometimes I get discouraged but remind myself that I'm doing this to make a better life for myself, and I love doing something out of the ordinary, seeing the sights, and being part of a team.

"Every crew is different as far as dietary needs, from gluten-free, vegetarian, allergies, or dislikes. It's a learning game, but I enjoy it.

"I've made some really good friends, both here and in other companies, like my friend Joanne from Canada. Joanne's wonderful, and we have our group, called *Cooks of the Great Lakes*, so we share our food ideas and recipes with each other, and they share with us. No matter how good you are you can never stop learning."

The cooks still live and work aboard the ship and they must receive the same safety training that the other sailors receive. Included below are some photos Kari provided of her Fire Fighting and Water Safety Training.

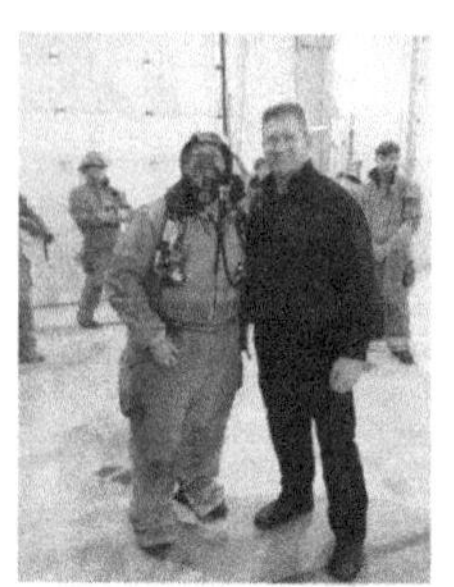

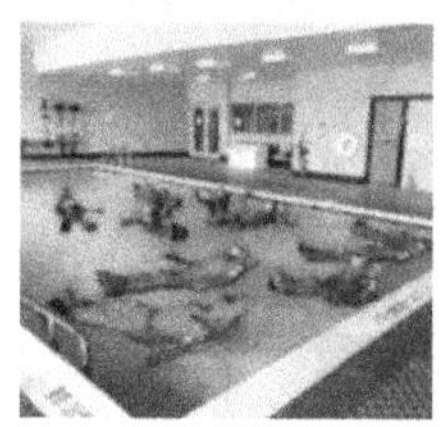

7

CATHERINE SCHMUCK

Catherine Schmuck is another member of the *Cooks of the Great Lakes* Facebook page, and she too agreed to contribute some stories about her sailing career for this book. Catherine is Canadian and lives in Mont-Tremblant, Quebec. She has sailed with several Canadian-flagged steamship companies such as the Canada Steamship Lines, Algoma Central Marine, Pioneer, and Misener. Catherine is also a published author[2]. The cookbook was published by her sister, Lorraine. Catherine's father was an accomplished photographer, and Catherine certainly inherited many of her father's talents with a camera, which is evidenced by the photographs in her book.

The middle child of three girls, Catherine says she and her sisters were in constant demand as babysitters for their neighbors. She took a job at a local motel/restaurant when she was fifteen, performing any of the jobs required. When the owners took family excursions on Sundays, Catherine ran the entire operation, from the office to the restaurant and bar. When she was nineteen, a male guest of the motel told her about the good money to be made aboard the Great

Lakes ships. Catherine was then able to convince her parents to let her, and her seventeen-year-old sister, attend the Seafarer's Training Institute in Morrisburg, Ontario.

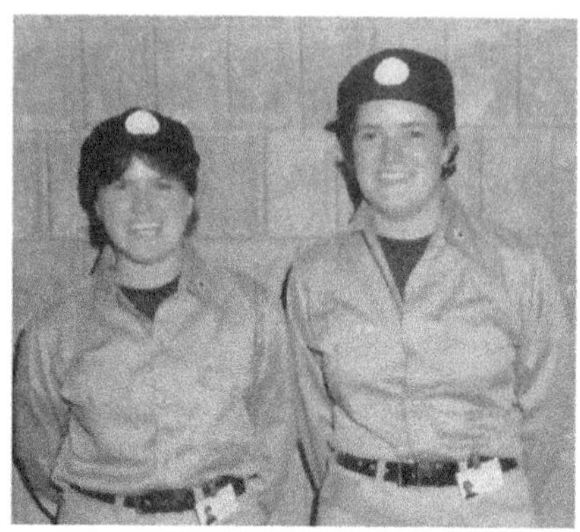

Catherine's sister, Lorraine was sent to a ship just 2 weeks after entering the training program, due to a serious shortage of mariners at that time. One week later, Catherine was meeting her first ship at Lock-1 in the Welland Canal, where she eventually became a night cook on the M/V Frontenac. That was back in 1981. She continued sailing until 1994.

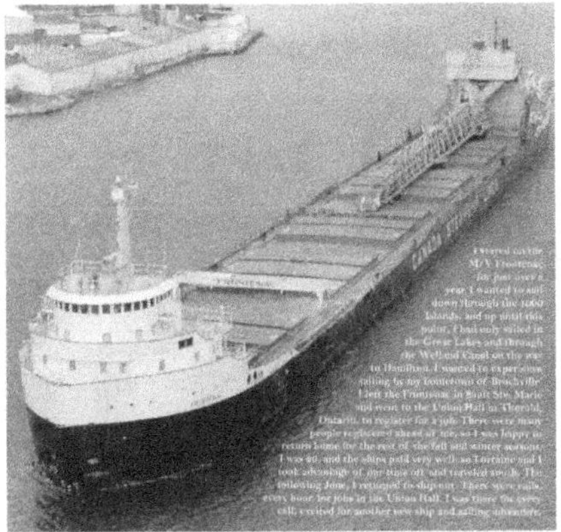

M/V Frontenac, photo from Catherine's
Cookbook.

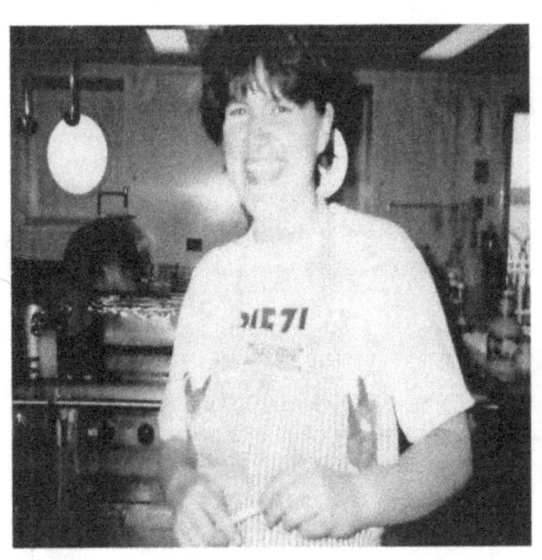

Over time, Catherine progressed from Porter to 2nd Cook, to Night Cook, and finally to Chief Cook, while aboard the *Louis R. Desmarais* in 1988. At the time, she was the youngest Chief Cook on the Lakes.

During her time ashore, Catherine started collecting cookbooks, as well as an unusual collection of chef figurines. In 1994, she left sailing and started her own restaurant ashore. But in 2019, Catherine decided to return to sailing. Sailing the Great Lakes had gotten into her blood.

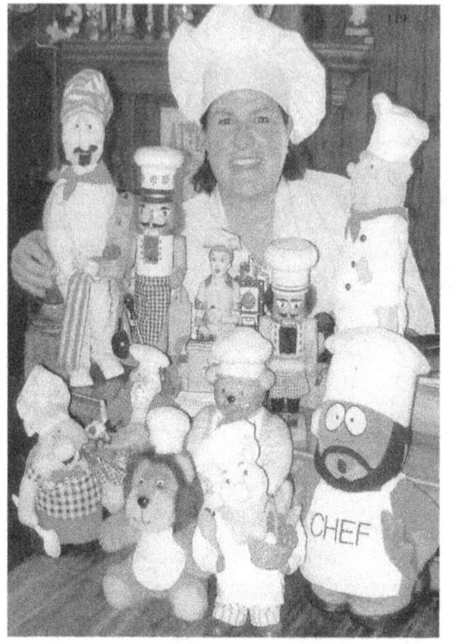

Catherine gets a great feeling of accomplishment when the crew members are happy after a good meal, she was responsible for preparing. Most Merchant Mariners are stuck aboard ship on Holidays, so preparing Thanksgiving, Christmas, and Easter dinner is always a big event onboard.

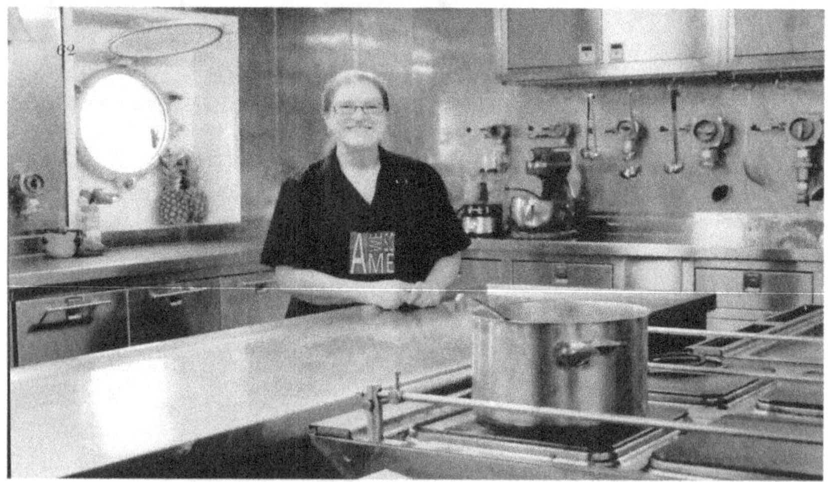

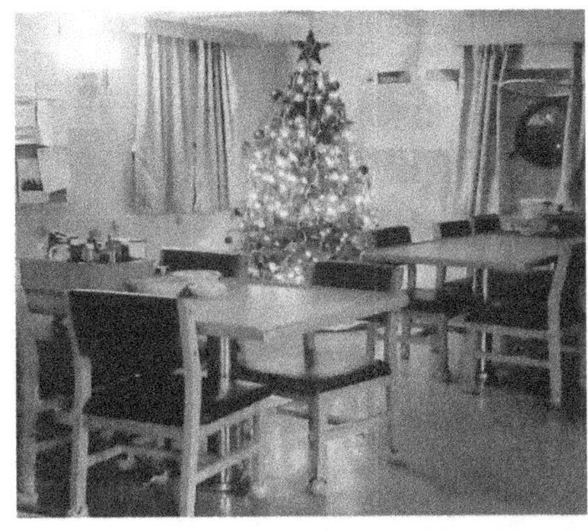

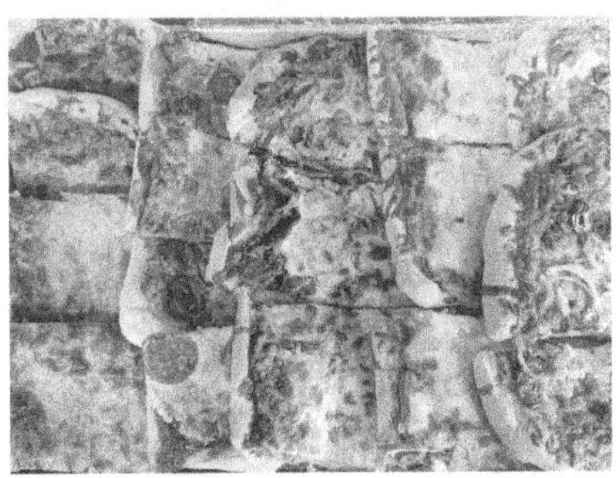

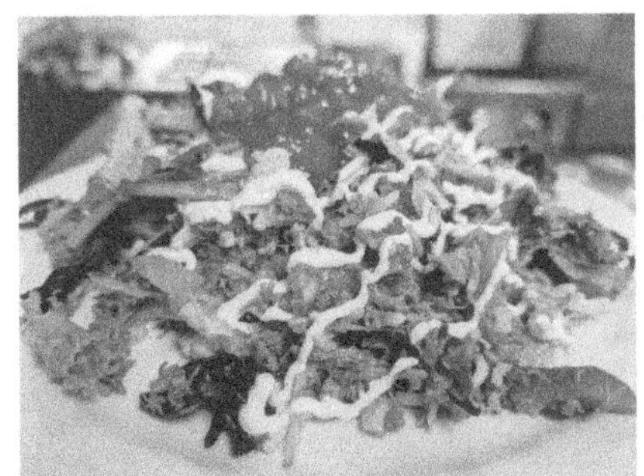

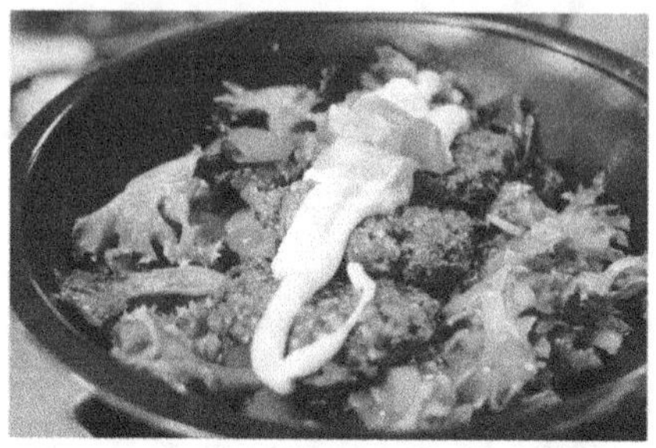

Look up Catherine's book, *Ship To Shore Chef*. It can be found at www.shiptoshorechef.com. It's not only a great cookbook, but also a beautifully crafted book, with wonderful photos of the Great Lakes, numerous ships, and of course, FOOD.

8

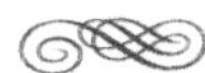

WHAT ABOUT THOSE MEN COOKS

Over the years, a majority of cooks in ship galleys have been men. Occasionally, a husband-and-wife team of cooks is spotted on the Great Lakes, but apart from being cooks on some carferries (and River towboats), women cooks were unusual, particularly on the Great Lakes. I was able to find a male cook, also a member of the Cooks of the Great Lakes Facebook page, willing to share his story of cooking on the Great Lakes.

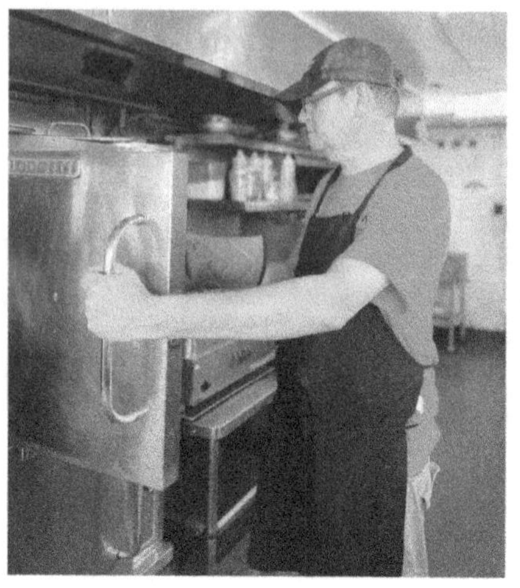

Jim Copek - A Most Unlikely Sailor

Had someone told me two years ago that I would be in my second season of cooking on the SS Badger, spending part of the winter between Badger seasons cooking on two of the largest ore boats on the Lakes during their winter lay-ups, I would have thought them delusional. But the pandemic caused so many people to make drastic life changes, including me.

My first experience with the Badger was some 25 years ago when in my previous career as a sales and service rep for food processing equipment, I had reason to take the Badger during one of its last crossings of the 1997 season. I had to be in Algoma, WI, on a Tuesday, and then in central Michigan the next day, so the Badger was the logical choice. That Monday night, the Packers were playing at home, so there were no hotel rooms to be found anywhere near where I needed to be in the morning. I ended up at a small resort with housekeeping cottages on the shore of the lake. I fell asleep to the sound of waves crashing and wondered what my crossing on the Badger would be like. It was rough!

Upon boarding, I went into the gift shop and found the crew putting merchandise back on the shelves. They explained that it had been so rough that they had to close the galley. I decided the best thing for me to do would be to rent a stateroom and buy some Dramamine from the nice lady in the gift shop and sleep my way across the lake.

My next experience was a few years later when I had to go from central Michigan to the Twin Cities. Upon arrival in Ludington, I thought it odd that the Badger was already in port, as it wasn't due for a few hours. The clerk at the ticket office explained that the next day's crossing had been canceled because they had taken on a load of "bad coal" that had to be shoveled out by hand and would take a few days. How often are travel plans upended by bad coal I wondered, as I spent the next 9 hours driving.

Fast forward to twenty years later and I find myself living in central Wisconsin. My plans to open a restaurant had been put on hold due to the pandemic, so it was time to look for a job. I'm not quite sure how I found out that the Badger was hiring cooks, and whether I would be able to live on board, but within a few days, I found myself hired and filling out all of the forms for mariner credentials, a TWIC card, and medical.

It was not an easy transition to work the hours required and live on a boat, but I stuck with it. The worst was when I was the night cook, and I tried to sleep during the day with a week of fog, and the whistle sounding every 2 minutes. By the middle of the summer, I had become accustomed to the long hours and shipboard life and found myself thinking I wanted to cook on a freighter. I realized cooking on a ship was a unique job, and that I was becoming very good at it.

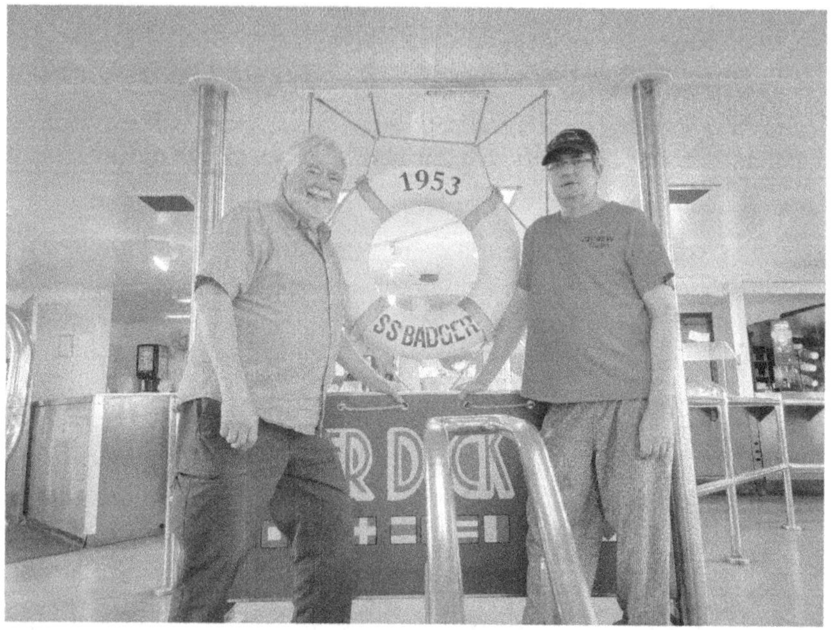

I had incredible support from the galley manager, and I credit her for making me a better cook and turning me into a sailor. Cooking on the Badger is unique for a Great Lakes vessel, because we have a much larger crew, and we are also cooking for the passengers. We have set very high standards for ourselves and sometimes the hours seem endless, but the compliments we get from both the crew and passengers put a spring in our step. I know our crew is now among the best fed on the Great Lakes.

It's not easy work, but it pays well and it's great to have a job that all my friends want to hear more about. Hopefully, I'll get the call to do relief galley work on the ore boats in the fall. In many ways, it's an easier gig than the Badger. When I was meeting the crew of the boats I cooked on during layup, I thought they might think that the Badger was not real sailing because we were in port every day and so on. On the contrary, they were amazed to find out that we went out to seas that would have them seeking shelter, and that we had an engineering department of twenty. A few younger crewmembers from the East Coast had no idea there was a cross-lake ferry service, and they were amazed that it was a nearly 70-year-old boat that was a coal-fired steamer.

Becoming a cook on the Great Lakes was a highly unlikely career choice, but now that I have done it for over a year, I can't see myself doing anything else.

9

WHAT ABOUT THE SPOUSES

Most relationships require constant nurturing, and marriages, where one spouse travels for work, can certainly pose their own challenges. This challenge becomes more compounded when one partner is regularly gone for sixty-plus days at a time. This absence, brought on by distance, can become a recipe for failure unless both of the people in the partnership understand the challenges and are prepared to work with the cards they've been dealt.

My father sailed the Great Lakes when I was growing up, so he was gone quite a lot. This was back in the "old days," when communication was archaic and not what it is . I share some of my parent's (especially my mother's) challenges in commentaries written throughout the stories shared below. Unfortunately, although communication channels have improved, conflicts arising from married sailors being gone, have not. And as I mentioned in the introduction, being gone for long periods does not only affect the homebound partner who now has to "run" everything while the sailor is gone, but it also affects the one sailing who then comes home, after being gone for months, and now wants everything to change back to his ways. It causes conflict because the homebound partner has been running the house, caring for any children, probably working in a career, and has a social life in clubs, volunteer work, or other organizations during the sailor's absence. And now, the sailor may want to have their partner's full attention while they are home. That just spells PROBLEMS!

In addition to my personal experience with my , I spoke with numerous wives and significant others of current sailors, to gain a more current understanding of the challenges, and the good times that come from being partnered with a Great Lakes Merchant Mariner. The first story is told by the wife of my friend, Ed Wiltse.

I met Ed Wiltse in Chicago when I was a member of the Great Lakes Shipmaster's Association. I had just started my own business as a Marine Surveyor, having left full-time employment as a surveyor for the American Bureau of Shipping. Ed was working on the Inland Steel fleet at the time. When he left Inland Steel and went to work for the owners of the Carferry Badger, they were converting the Carferry City of Midland 41 into a cargo barge, pushed by a tugboat.

The carferry to barge conversion was being done in Muskegon, and during that time, I made a few trips up to Ludington and Muskegon, bringing my family along on one of those trips. Having grown up in the "North Woods," I was never into camping (my early life was like a full-time camping trip) but my wife wanted us to camp at the State Park north of Ludington. We brought our tent, and I told Ed Wiltse about our plans. Unfortunately, there was a very unseasonable, heavy downpour when we arrived in Ludington, so camping in a tent was not in the cards. Ed & Anita Wiltse owned a pop-up camper trailer, and Ed came to the rescue, offering us the use of their trailer.

That's when I met Anita Wiltse for the first time. But I had heard so much about her from Ed, and he always spoke so highly of her. So, I decided to ask sailors' wives and/or partners to contribute their stories for this sequel to Sweetwater Sailors, Ed was the first person I contacted. I asked if he could ask Anita if she would be willing to contribute to the book.

Not only was Anita willing to write her story, but she also organized a meeting between the rest of the contributors (Connie Adamson, Ann Bell, Brenda Hobbs) to this section, their spouses, and me. So, much of this section was made possible with Anita's help and organization.

Anita Wiltse

Being Married to a Sailor:

I met Ed back in 1984 while both of us were in college. He was attending the Great Lakes Maritime Academy (GLMA) and I was attending Northwestern Michigan College (NMC). However, we didn't officially start dating until the spring of 1987. When he graduated with his merchant mariners license that same summer, he went out on his first licensed job with Oglebay Norton and was gone for months, until late winter.

We had been dating for only a couple of months and had been discussing being in a committed relationship. I knew he was going to be gone a lot, but we still decided to give it a shot. It was difficult right off the bat. My single friends would invite me to places out on the town, but there were many times when I wouldn't go. Occasionally, however, I wanted to go out dancing with them, and felt so guilty, even though I wasn't doing anything wrong. I was young and didn't want to wait for months for him to return. I understand that he chose this career path but now I wasn't so sure if I wanted to sign up for this type of lifestyle. I was pretty naive about the level of commitment being linked to his career required. Needless to say, we split up.

Months later, a mutual friend informed me that Ed had accepted a new captain's position on a tug-barge operation at the Inland Steel

Plant, which meant he would be home in the evenings and not gone for 90-plus days - it was a regular job!

I pondered this exciting news for a couple of weeks, trying to decide whether or not to phone him. I figured he'd tell me to go take a hike. But we cautiously decided that our relationship was worth giving a second chance. Thank goodness! We have been married for 32 years and counting!

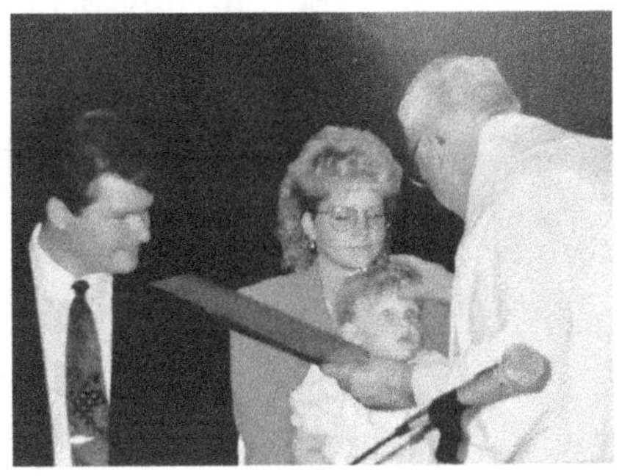

Of course, as was to be expected, Ed's career as a sailor has evolved over the years we've been married. He's been gone sailing, on and off as a mate or captain for different companies for more than half of our marriage. However, living a life together in 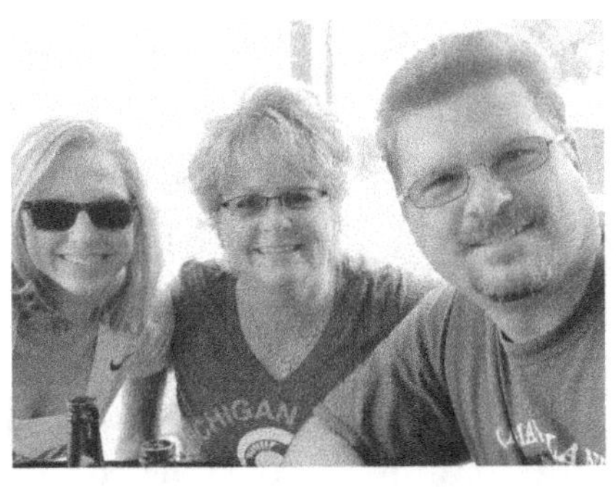 short-term increments can be quite tricky. I believe you must be independent and somewhat strong to put up with the hardships that inevitably come with this crazy lifestyle. While I don't want to come across as complaining, it can be very daunting and exhausting at times. Working my own career, raising a daughter, running a household, and trying to keep a social life are just a few examples.

While I juggled all these areas of life back home, Ed was able to be more carefree with his time. When he had multiple days off from the ship, I still had to work my full-time job as a CAD Draftsperson. The reality was that my employer depended on me as well, so it was difficult to take time off with meetings and deadlines when Ed was home. I was thrilled to have him home and would've loved to run around all day or go on a vacation, but I only had two vacation weeks per year, so they had to be carefully planned. I was always torn and conflicted.

Back then, there were no cell phones, FaceTime, or social media. No call waiting or answering machines. Just a dirty pay phone in a spidery phone booth at the docks (that was how he would explain it to me). So, if I wasn't home to answer his phone calls, I might not speak to him until they got to the next port, which could be a few days or up to a week. Then, I would forget to tell him things because last week's news was old news. I would be upset with myself if I missed his calls. He missed out on some of our daughter's milestones, like crawling, talking, walking, and later, the dreaded dating.

I was the main disciplinarian for our daughter and tended to her daily needs and routines. I would get a little perturbed when Ed came home and would try to change things up by being the fun dad. That would last for a short time because our daughter was always so happy to see him and spend time with him, which made me happy for them. Even though he was the boss on the ship, it was hard for him not to be the boss at home.

Running a household and trying to keep things in order while working full-time and raising a child is very exhausting. The daily tasks such as paying bills, making doctor appointments, household repairs, grocery shopping, cooking, cleaning, laundry, mowing, raking, and shoveling, and too many more to list, is most definitely not a fun job!

Trying to keep up with a social life can be a huge challenge.

Having traditional couple friends that don't necessarily understand the sailor's wife's lifestyle, you can sometimes feel like a fifth wheel when they ask you to join them for dinner. So sometimes, I would graciously make excuses to bail out. When it comes to meeting friends who are in the industry, they understand inclusiveness when the partner is away, and the missing in action (MIA) when husbands are home, better than non-maritime friends do.

Regular traditional (non-maritime) couples don't understand the lifestyle. They do things as couples and that's great when your husband is off the ship, but they don't want a 'single' woman hanging around while they are doing things as couples. They also don't understand that when your husband is home, you're going to want to be MIA for a couple of weeks. These challenges lead to roller-coaster friendships that eventually fade out. Single friends are the best to have outside of having 'couple' friends in the industry.

Despite the challenges, I have many positive memories from being part of the maritime industry, things the average "shoreside" person would never get to experience. For instance, I was blessed to take a few Lake and River trips with Ed before we had our daughter, Erika. It has provided a nice living for us, and thankfully we've had the time to build a great foundation for a stable relationship. Not to say that it's perfect, but we're pretty content and happy. (Bob's comment – You beat the average for the length of most marriages.)

Back in the day, before homeland security was so prominent and strict, one of the myths associated with being a sailor was that male sailors had a woman in every port. I witnessed a reaction to this myth from a dock boss when Ed and I came back from going 'up the street' while in port, and he thought I was one of 'those gals' that Ed was bringing back to the ship. He was telling Ed to have fun and kept winking at him. Ed told him I was his wife, and he was saying, 'Yeah, sure, I understand.' I thought it was pretty funny.

One of the few boat trips I took was on the SS *Wilfred Sykes*.

It was a fun and interesting five-day trip that few outsiders get to experience. It was a unique inside look at Ed's job duties while standing watch and loading the ship.

Unloaded and light, while going under the Mackinac bridge, it felt like I could reach up and touch the bottom of the Mighty Mac. It didn't seem so high above the water like being in a car and traveling over the bridge. It was pretty impressive to see it from that perspective.

Ed's shipmates were nice and pleasant to be around and seemed to be on their best behavior. Ginny was a cook and the only female on the ship. Eating time was amazing, especially with the wide variety of food, anytime, day or night. It was homemade comfort food and fresh baked goods. A time to relax and enjoy, as I was a glutton for their desserts. I could see why the crew looked forward to eating. Ginny took me under her wing for a few days while I was aboard. She secretly offered me a used sexy teddy drenched in perfume, which I politely declined. Although her heart was in the right place, it was a bit awkward.

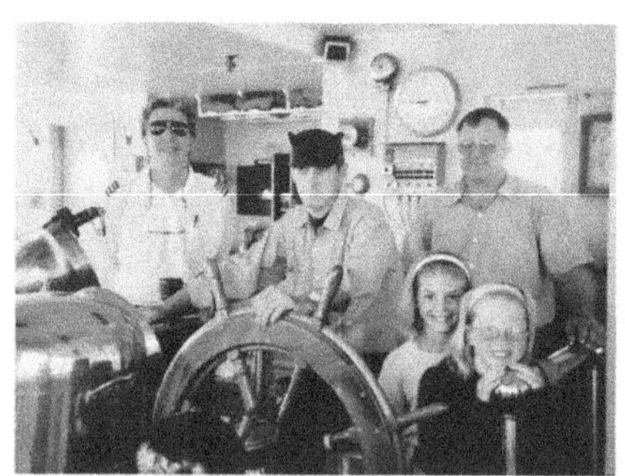

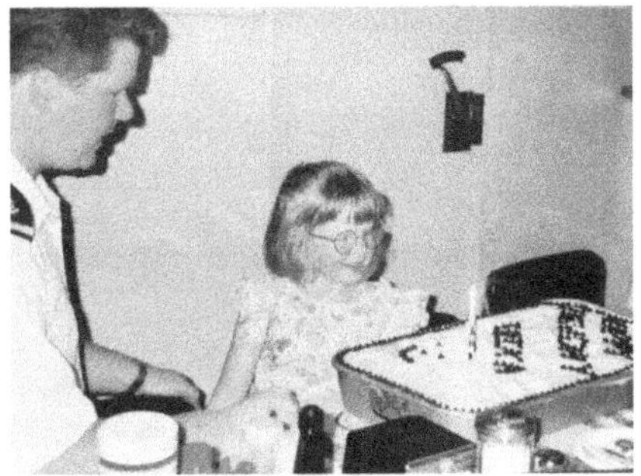

One of my favorite memories aboard a ship was when our daughter, Erika, celebrated her fifth birthday on the SS *Badger*. Ed was a mate at the time, and Captain Dean Hobbs was a family friend, which meant that we were treated like royalty. When we arrived in Manitowoc, Wisconsin, he took us to the local chocolate shop for some ice cream and chocolate. When we got back to the *Badger*, the kitchen crew had baked Erika a surprise birthday cake, and Captain Dean gave up his quarters so Erika and I could have movie night and eat popcorn while Ed was working. We occasionally took some day trips on the *Badger*, and Erika was able to bring along her friend, Korinne.

10

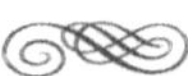

ANITA WILTSE – CAMARADERIE

Wives, and partners of anyone in atypical careers, have problems relating to people who consider themselves as leading "normal" lives. When I (the Author) was traveling the world in my marine surveying career, my wife was frustrated when our neighbors asked her where I was. She told them I was in Guam, or Sicily, or Japan, and she would tell me, "They think you left me and I'm just making up stories." I share this to let you know that I understand this section because of my own personal experiences.

Anita Wiltse

Being raised in Marine City, Michigan, a small maritime town on the shores of the Saint Clair River, in the mid-'60s, it wasn't unusual to see and hear the salutes of the freighters heading up-bound or down-bound as they passed by one another day or night. Many locals and even some of my relatives worked on the freighters, as did my father for a short stint on the *SS Robert C. Stanley*. It was a decent-paying job and a way of life.

In the early '70s, due to my father's job transfer, we moved 250 miles north to Kalkaska, Michigan, another small town far removed from maritime life. But I still had relatives back in Marine City, so most of our family vacations were spent there.

It's in my blood - I LOVE the sight and sound of the freighters! But fast forward to the mid-80s - I met a Merchant Cadet in a maritime town in Traverse City, Michigan, while he was attending GLMA, and we married in his hometown of Portage, Indiana.

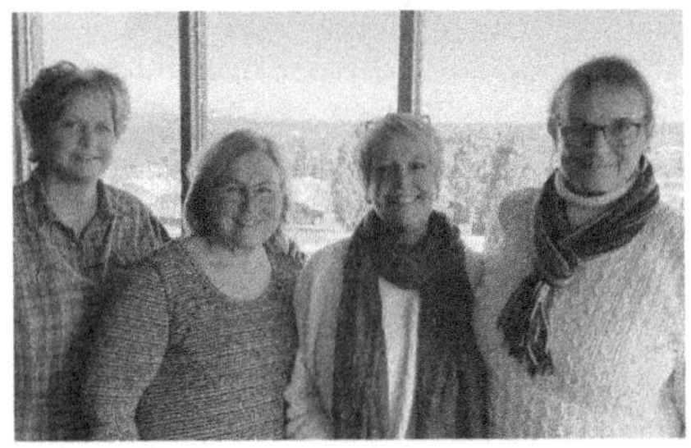

Traverse City, Michigan (TC), is a maritime town with a lot of GLMA graduates, many of whom decide to stay, marry, and raise families in the city where they attended college.

It's a small industry, and a lot of the boat wives know one another through different maritime functions, and they would typically become fast friends. I feel it is an unwritten understanding/rule that we look out for one another because we all understand the crazy and ridiculous lifestyle.

When my husband, Ed, was off the ships, he would help the other boat widows with household repairs/chores or car problems, and their husbands would do the same for me. Most important to me, while their husbands are on the ship, is to include the boat widows in our plans, whether it's dinner, movies, or gatherings, where they are comfortable enough not to feel like a fifth wheel. One of the fun things Ed and I would do was host dinners on Sundays for either our stray friends off the ships and/or boat widows. We would laugh, eat, drink and catch up. A fun, harmless night for all.

Usually, the fit-out of the fleet and spring break for the kids were around the same time, so it was never a possibility to go away as a family for spring break vacation. My friend, Connie, who also was a boat widow, and her daughter, Kelly, who is the same age as my daughter, Erika, and I came up with a new tradition and planned our spring breaks together. We had some really fun girl trips. We made a few days out to the Mall of America in Minneapolis and spent a week in Mexico, as well as some local Michigan trips to Grand Rapids.

I (the author) can sympathize with these authors' references to the 'Camaraderie of Boat Widows' because my mother did not live in a town with other 'Boat Widows', and led a lonely social life as a result. Those circumstances eventually led to my parents' early divorce.

11

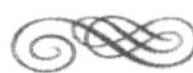

CONNIE ADAMSON

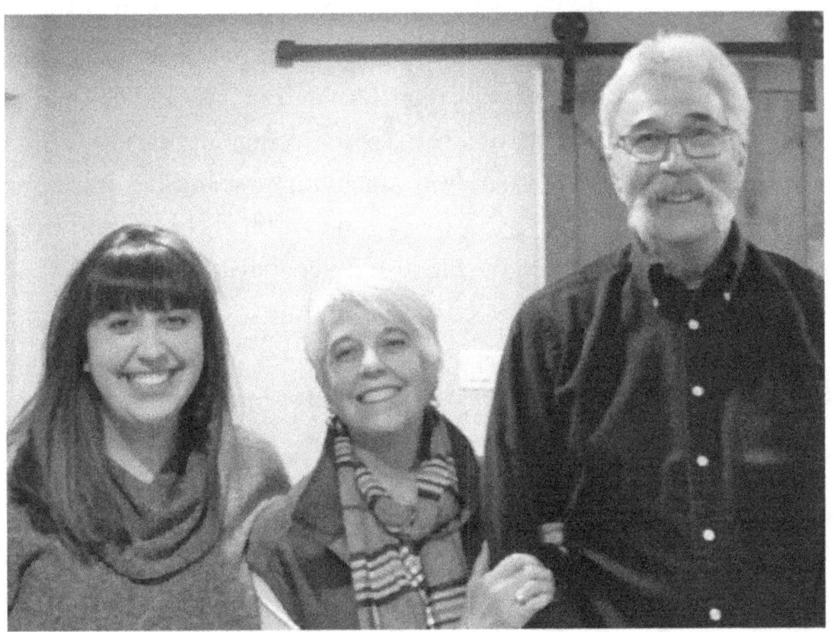

My name is Connie Adamson, and I've been married to Mark Adamson for 34 years. Mark sailed the Great Lakes for 45 years and retired as a Captain from the American Steamship Company. We live in Traverse City, Michigan. I grew up in Iowa and lived in Minneapolis in my 20s, so I had never really heard much about maritime life. We met through a mutual friend and dated for about a month before he had to go back on the boats. When I dropped him off at the airport, he was very quiet and wouldn't even hug me goodbye (which I thought was very hurtful!). I went home and called my sister to vent, and luckily, she told me that he was probably concerned I wouldn't still be around when he returned! I later found out that was true, it had happened to him before.

I think one of the hardest things about maritime life back then was such little communication. Letters took a while, and sometimes we would go ten days without talking. When in port, all the guys wanted to use the phone booth, so they would have to stand in line in all kinds of weather (day or night), then have just a little time to talk so everyone could have a turn. Being young and new to this, I have to admit that I wasn't always really understanding...until one time when he was home, and I was gone and had to call him from an outside phone in the pouring rain. I kept saying I had to go due to the weather, but he just talked on and on...smart man, 'cause I finally got it!

Another thing I had to learn was to give him three days before I brought up any serious conversation, as he needed to sleep and decompress into "home reality" vs "boat reality". Then, switch it around for the last three days of the vacation...nothing serious the last three days because he was in what we called "boat mode," emotionally changing gears.

Purchasing, running, and maintaining a home (both indoors and outdoors) and cars, completely alone, can be a bit overwhelming. So, you just have to be organized and have a routine. Once "the captain" came home and wanted to take over or change that routine...well, let's just say there may have been some angry words spoken to the tune of "you may be the captain on the boat but I'm the captain here!" Then along comes an only child who thinks she is the one in charge (which, let's face it, she was quite a bit of the time!), so when we got our first email, it had to start with "captains3."

Luckily, Mark was home for the birth of our daughter, Kelly. I'm not sure if it was harder on him or me when he left three weeks later. He missed a lot of "milestones," and we celebrated a lot of holidays on different dates, but the nice thing was that when he was home, he was home...24/7 the whole time.

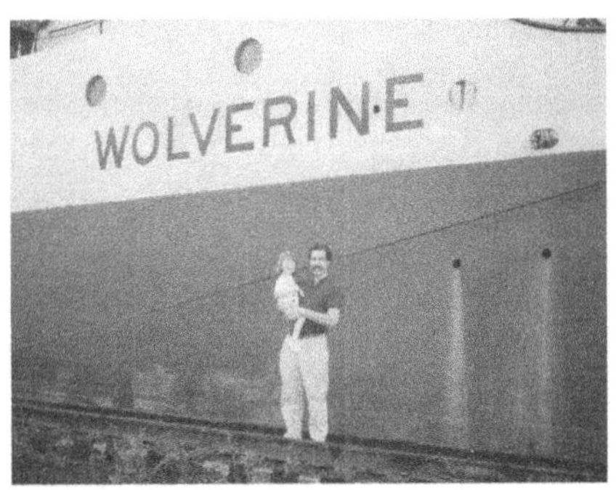

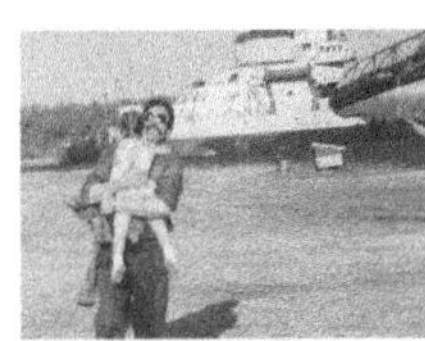
Being a "married yet single" woman was interesting. In social situations, many times, married couples would want to get together only when Mark was around, and my single friends wanted to go out to bars (which I loved in my 20s but not after marriage and a baby!)

Luckily, I knew a few other maritime wives who understood the lifestyle... we could be supportive of one another and go on spring break together. That, along with being very involved in the school and our church, kept me going!

Both partners must be strong and independent, or this lifestyle just won't work. Those on the boats have a tough job and the hardship of not seeing their family often. Those at home have to deal with many things they don't want to, but there is just no one else around to do them! When Mark retired, I put off retirement for another year and a half...I was a little concerned about being together all the time! But we quickly adjusted and it's a joy to share everyday life and everyday responsibilities.

12

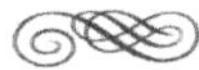

ANN BELL

*Most of the contributors to Sweetwater Sailors, and this sequel, have given me short snippets of their experiences in the Maritime Industry. Ann Bell told me she has wanted to write her story, about her life as a **Boat Widow**, for a long time. When I first received her story and saw how long it was, I thought it might be too much for a book like this. But then I read the story! I saw why Ann felt she needed to share it, and I loved it!*

Allan Bell is a First Mate, sailing with the Interlake Steamship Company. This first picture is of Allan and his mother, taken when she visited Allan aboard one of the ships.

As I've mentioned, I am the product of a Boat Widow family. My parents divorced after just fifteen years, and I could recognize many of the problems my parents experienced, contained in Ann Bell's story. As Ann says in her first paragraph, "Being a Maritime family is in every sense of the word, unique."

I will add occasional commentary to help guide the reader, but I suggest that Ann's story should be read from start to finish when the reader has time to absorb the whole experience of what it is really like to be part of a Maritime family. Most people could never handle it all and remain a couple!

So, here's Ann's story (I added all the headers, except for the first one).

Ann's Story: At one time, I said I was going to write a book and gather all the Maritime women to also share their stories. I even had the title: "I married a Freighter, Dedicated to the Maritime Women of the Past, Present, and Future." I had the opportunity to meet Bob Ojala this past fall, and he asked me to share my story. I wish I had taken the time to journal over the years, but I'm sure each of us will share our own unique story. Being a Maritime family is in every sense of the word, 'unique'.

<u>The beginning - Before we knew anything about the Maritime Industry</u>

I met my husband, Allan, in September 1984 in Orillia, Ontario, Canada, at an engagement party. I didn't know a single person other than my childhood friend, who was the one who asked me to go to Canada with her. While at the party, I saw this cute guy off to the side, and later that evening we started talking. By the end of the evening, I decided that I was interested in getting to know him. I remember returning home from the weekend and telling my mom that I met the guy I was going to marry.

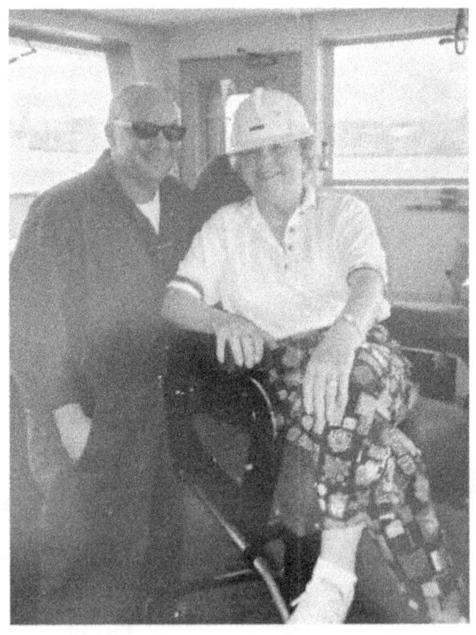

Allan lived in Toronto, and I lived with my parents five hours away in a west-side suburb of Detroit. Later that fall, I invited Allan to come for the weekend so we could go to a Lions game. My dad had season tickets and was happy to give up his seats for us to attend the game. After that weekend, Allan returned home, and we talked to each other often. Our phone bills were ridiculous, and it wasn't long before we started taking turns commuting to see each other. Little did I know that this was just a glimpse of the life that a long-distance relationship would be like. You see, every time we got together, it was a fun time. We would go to area attractions, and restaurants, visit each other's friends and families and pack as much as we could into a weekend when we were together. From Friday to Sunday, we spent at least 8 hours commuting, and don't forget the delays at the International Bridge, getting through customs, which wasn't always fast. We took the train back and forth, then we just decided that flying would add more time to our visits. It was expensive, but it was worth it. We couldn't wait until the next time when saw each other again.

In June of 1985, we were engaged. We started to plan the wedding, and since I was a nurse, we initially planned for me to get my nursing License in Canada and I would move there. Then Allan thought that maybe it would be better for him to move to Michigan because he thought it would be easier for me since I had never lived on my own and I was very close to my family. We had to go through the legal immigration red tape and interrogations. However, it went pretty smoothly and we were able to get past that quickly. Allan left a great job at a very large Fire Equipment Company in Toronto and moved to Michigan on a Fiancé Petition in January 1986. Allan wasn't in the country a whole day when we received news that my mom had been diagnosed with Breast Cancer. She passed away two years later in 1988, and this was such a blow and such an emotional time. I remember being so thankful for Allan wanting to move to Michigan, as I couldn't imagine not being there for my parents and family during this time. He was a great comfort to me and so supportive. This was our first trial of many over the years.

I became Mrs. Bell on Sept 27, 1986. Allan looked for employment, something like the job he had left in Canada, but soon found out that they were not the same in Michigan. In Canada, the company he had worked for paid him a good salary with benefits, but in Michigan, the fire equipment companies were usually small, family-owned businesses that paid minimum wage with no benefits and no room for advancement. During the first few years, Allan did various jobs to make ends meet and took classes at our local community college. He was always looking in the paper for a potential job opportunity that would become a future career."

<u>Off to the Maritime Academy</u>

It all started in March of 1991, in the Detroit News' help wanted ads. Allan noticed a silhouette of a ship and a 1-800 number. This piqued Allan's interest, and he followed up with a phone call. He was invited to attend a local recruitment seminar from The Great Lakes Maritime Academy. Allan returned home from the local seminar with more knowledge, which led both of us to have a more serious conversation about Allan pursuing a career in the Maritime Industry.

We had some hard conversations about uprooting and leaving the Detroit area, but we knew that after he finished school, we could go back. I thought to myself that we survived our long-distance relationship when he lived in Toronto, and I was the daughter of a Detroit Fireman. So, I grew up with my dad gone most of the time because when he wasn't at the station, he was working a second job on his days off. Many times, it would be every other Sunday when I would see my dad. Allan and I both said that we should consider this opportunity, so the next step was to take a 4-hour trip north to Traverse City and meet with the Great Lakes Maritime Academy Recruiter, Mr. Grimm.

On the way back home, we had further discussions about the pros and cons. I knew how important it was for Allan to have a career and to be able to provide for his family. Allan needed my support, so we both decided to take a chance on our future. The recruiter, Mr. Grimm, did a good job because when we returned home, we set things in motion. We made this commitment, and it was fast and furious, exciting, and scary all at the same time. At times I felt an overwhelming sense of doom and fear of the unknown setting in. At times I also said to myself, 'What did I do?' trying to convince myself I was ready for a change.

In May of 1991, Allan moved to Traverse City to start school, and I stayed behind with our then 2-year-old son, Andrew, to prepare our home to be put on the market. I was working full time and had to manage all the household duties and pack with any spare time I had. We would see each other when I could make a trip up for the weekend, so we were in a long-distance relationship once again. We finally sold our home in September and joined Allan in our cozy little 2-bedroom apartment. While Allan attended school, I worked the afternoon shift at the hospital in Traverse City. This schedule worked out perfectly because it allowed Allan to be at school during the day, and he was able to study after he put Andrew to bed. Most days of the week, we were two ships passing in the night, rarely seeing each other.

Comradery Amongst the Cadets

Allan was older than the majority of his classmates. He was 31 when he went back to school, so we became the mom and dad of some of the Cadets. They were so young at ages 18, 19, and 20. Allan connected with several of the cadets, and they formed a study group, spending a lot of time together, and we became good friends. They were fun to be around. We hosted Thanksgiving and Christmas for the Cadets that didn't make it home. Soon we became a big family, and we looked out for one another. We even became "Bell's Bail Bonds" for those who got into hot water and didn't want their folks to know.

Sometimes, Allan could be the dad of the Cadets, but I can tell you, he didn't always act his age. I did see digression to an 18, 19, or 20-year-old in my husband, especially when he would get together for a Saturday afternoon study session. I later learned that it was a board game, Axis and Allies Marathon Tournament. Often the Cadets would visit, and I remember one nice sunny afternoon when two of the Cadets stopped by to talk to Allan. I didn't think anything of it, but the next thing I knew, they took Andrew. I asked

Allan, 'Where did they go? To the park?' Allan replied, 'No, they took him to the mall.' I said, 'To the Mall? Why would they want to take him to the Mall?' Allan looked at me and said, 'Imagine two young, good-looking guys in uniform with a 2-year-old. They took him for *Chick Bait*. Don't worry, he'll be fine.'

In 1992, Allan's second year of school, we purchased a home in the dead smack of winter, and we moved during a blustery blizzard! I'm forever thankful that we were able to take advantage of young strong men (cadets) who helped us move. All I had to do was feed them!

Later that spring, I was so exhausted, and I chalked it up to being a 'single mom' for much of the time, working full time, with a preschooler, and the work that came with being a homeowner. I remember while at work one evening, I was telling a co-worker how exhausted I was, and how I didn't ever remember being so exhausted, other than the time I was pregnant with Andrew. Well, the light bulb began shining bright this time. Oh my God, I could be pregnant!

Well, my anticipation couldn't wait, and the next morning, after two home pregnancy tests, I found out that I was! I was so shocked and excited. I couldn't wait to tell Allan. Allan was on a ship for his annual Sea Project training. I remember calling the satellite phone on the ship and asking the Captain to have Allan return an urgent call, not an emergency call. Allan called home when he had a few minutes to talk, and I shared our news. I can still remember how excited he was. All we wanted to do was jump through the phone and hug each other!

<u>Fitting In Visits Where & When Possible</u>
I can identify with Ann's story here because my mother would pack up my sister and me, drive up to Port Inland, Michigan, and sit on the dock

at night waiting for my father's ship to arrive. We sometimes also took a carferry across Lake Michigan to see my father for just a few hours while his ship was unloading.

A few weeks passed by, and then Allan called home, saying that his boat would be in Lorain, Ohio. We both thought how great it would be to spend a little time together, bonding with our son and sharing the joy of our news. By this time, I had morning sickness, or all-day sickness is what I call it, because every waking second, I was nauseated. All I wanted to do was lay down and sleep because this was the only time when I didn't feel sick. I knew how important it was for us to be together, but I wasn't sure how I'd get through this pregnancy without my husband being home. I packed the necessary things, and off we went to Lorain. I traveled six hours from Traverse city with a barf bag by my side and a preschooler who wasn't thrilled to be in his car seat. In the end, I knew it would be worth it.

Time was of the essence, and when we arrived in Lorain, the boat wasn't there. The boat was delayed because **'boats always get delayed'**. We drove around for hours it seemed, because I wasn't getting out of the car in that neighborhood. Finally, Allan's boat arrived. We barely got to spend much time together before he had to return in a few hours to report to duty. We tried to find a hotel nearby, but everything in that county was booked, except for the local den of iniquity, pay by the hour, down the road. I was exhausted, morning sickness was taking its toll, and our preschooler just had an accident. Allan said in a calm, reassuring voice, 'We'll just go to the pay-by-the-hour hotel, and it'll be OK.'

Allan obtained the room key, and we entered this nasty, and I mean NASTY, room. I cleaned Andrew up the best I could without either of us touching a thing. Thank God I had a blanket in the car to put down on that skuzzy bed, so we would have something non-contaminated to lay on. We didn't even take our shoes off. We had just nodded off, it seemed, and I heard Allan gently call my name,

'Ann, wake up. Ann, wake up. Don't say a word. When I tell you to get in the car, just get in the car. Don't ask questions. Just get in the car. As soon as you're in the car, I'm going to hand Andrew to you. We're getting the hell out of here.' Apparently, there was a drug/prostitute situation gone wrong a few rooms down, and it was escalating. Allan drove out of there like a bat out of hell, and once Allan felt safe, a little way down the road, he pulled over to put Andrew in his car seat. The next words out of Allan's mouth, which I already knew, 'You might as well drop me off at the boat; I have to report in an hour anyway.' We said our disappointing goodbyes, and I was back on the road.

I drove until I saw signs of the sunrise, and I pulled over at a gas station. I put my quarter in the phone and placed a call to my brother, who lived outside of Detroit, and asked him if I could come to his house and get a little sleep while he watched Andrew. I just had to get some sleep before heading back to Traverse City. It was one of the downsides of being a Maritime wife: not all the times are "Mari" (merry).

A Growing Family

Our daughter, Lauren, was born at the end of Feb 1993. I ended up having a post-operative infection from my C-section, which landed me in the hospital for an extra week. All I wanted to do was come home and be with my husband and son, but I was too sick. While in the hospital, I received many visits from some of the Cadets. I didn't know what was funnier, hearing things like 'Does Allan have a shotgun ready? He's going to be waiting on the porch with his gun in hand.' or watching their reaction when they held a newborn baby or the ones who clearly were very uncomfortable with the thought of holding something so fragile. They were so thoughtful and brought flowers for me, a gift for the new baby, and cigars for Allan. We even had some of the cadets' girlfriends come by to congratulate us. Once I was discharged from the hospital and returned home, it didn't take long for everything to fall into place, and things started to feel somewhat normal.

That didn't last long, as May came too quickly, and Allan was looking forward to graduation. We were all feeling the stress of his upcoming departure. I thought I was going to lose it, or perhaps I did. I was still on Maternity Leave, with a new baby, and a now active, almost 4-year-old, and with no family to rely on. I was beginning to know what a pity party was, and I wasn't certain how I was going to navigate all of this without Allan. I spent many moments just bursting into tears.

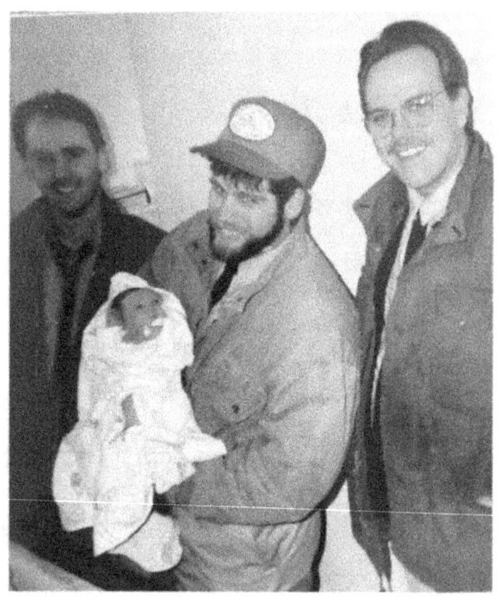

Allan was about to graduate from the Academy and prepare for his Licensing exams, but little did we know that there was a huge snag in the plan. The thing was, Allan was not a U.S. citizen, which meant that he could not sail on the Great Lakes. This topic never came up, and it was not on our radar that this would even be a requirement. So, Allan had to apply for Immigration to become a citizen. For weeks, we anxiously awaited a response. Time passed, and we had not heard back from the immigration office. Meanwhile, the exam deadline was fast approaching, so Allan called our state representative, hoping to find answers and speed things up. Fortunately, it worked! Allan received his Citizenship just in time to take and pass his licensing exam. We celebrated when he received his license. Allan's mom even came down from Canada, and my dad came from Florida. It was a proud moment for all of us.

<u>...Then the Actual Job Starts</u>

Allan and I decided to remain in Traverse City and make it our forever home. Allan was in four Maritime weddings and we became lifelong friends with some of the Cadets, their wives, and their children. We became Godparents of some. Although we are not blood-related, we are family, and there isn't anything that we wouldn't do for each other. And to this day, it remains the same.

It wasn't long before Allan got a job and had to leave. The work schedule was 60 days on and 30 days off, but it was more likely for him to be gone 90 days at a time. Our only way to communicate was by "snail mail," which was the US post office, or by Allan finding a phone booth at the dock to make a call. I never knew when he would be able to call or what time of day or night it would come. I remember when we didn't have an answering machine, and call-waiting didn't even exist back then. I would put the kids to bed around 8 o'clock. After they fell asleep, I would get on the phone with friends and family from back home, which meant it was a long-distance call. Our phone bills were high, but a small price to pay when I missed them too.

When the kids were little, the evenings were the loneliest for me.

It might be weeks before Allan could call me. Sometimes he would call in the middle of the night after walking a few blocks to a phone booth in a snowstorm, only to wait in line until it was his turn. At one time, I thought he purposely didn't call me for a long time. When we were finally able to connect, I let him HAVE IT! Why haven't you called, I can't believe it's been this long. Oh yes, he was getting an earful. I'm sure other maritime wives can relate. All of a sudden, after I got all of my frustrations out, I heard a click at the other end. Dead silence. Well, see there, I thought to myself, I hope he gets it now, and he better not wait that long to call me again! It was a while before I heard from him again, and this time while on the phone, he said, 'I will not ever call home again if this is all that I am going to get from you on the other end! Every time I tried to call you, the phone was busy!'

Communication was a challenge. We didn't have the conveniences of today's world. We were so happy for Christmas that year when my dad gifted us an answering machine. That helped so much because Allan would call home even if he knew I wouldn't be there. He could leave a message when he thought he could call again. When call-waiting was available, we added that to our phone plan.

Keeping The Kids Happy

When the kids were a little older, weekends became lonely too. Weekends were for family time for most, so we had to make our own fun. In the summer, we would often go to a local beach, but that got boring after a while. One weekend, I rented a cabin at a local campground for the kids to experience camping life. Lauren was 3, and Andrew was 7. We brought bikes, games, and all the necessities. We all had a great time, and the kids saw a new side of life outdoors. When we were able to share our experience with Allan, he was truly happy for us. I was so excited, and I told him that we were going to get a tent and all that went with it. I had it all planned, but as I was telling him, he stopped me before all my excitement ended. He said we are not getting a tent. All it would take is one good rain and that would end the fun for all of you! I think you would be safer in a pop-up and have more room if the weather wasn't good. That year we got a pop-up, and two weekends out of the month; while Allan was gone, the kids and I packed up and took off for the weekend. It really helped with the loneliness. We had that pop-up for 26 years.

In the winter, we joined Hickory Hills, a City-run, tow-rope-only ski hill. That is where the kids and I self-taught and learned to ski. Allan, being from Canada, was an excellent skier! It was five minutes from home to the ski hill. I got out of work at four, the kids did their homework, had dinner, and then we hit the hill for an hour or two and be home by 8. We had a blast, and when Allan came home, he joined us for the fun. One thing about being a Maritime wife, I learned that I had to make my own fun for the kids, and I couldn't depend on others. So now, I added another role to my Maritime wifehood, being the CEO of our children's entertainment committee.

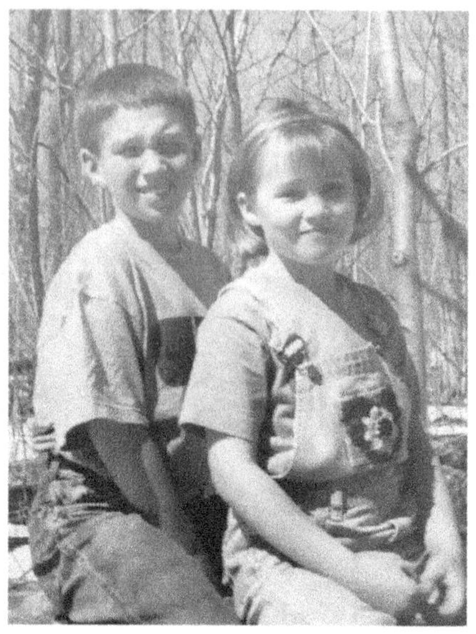

At times, we would take a trip across to Alpena to see Allan when his boat came in. We would pack a lunch, go to a park, and visit for a few hours. 'A little time was better than no time' became my motto. Allan called one time and said he thought his boat would be coming into Port Inland and he would have a little time off. It wasn't a for-sure thing, so he said to make sure I call WLC (single side-band radio station) before I left because his orders could change. Well, I got a little excited, loaded the kids up, and drove 5-hours (over the Mackinac Bridge) to Port Inland. When we arrived, there wasn't a boat in sight. After about thirty minutes of waiting, I made my way closer to the water with the kids in tow, anxiously waiting to see their daddy. I saw someone who worked there, and I inquired about the status. He used his radio only to confirm that Allan's orders had been changed, and I hadn't done what Allan told me to do.

I remember being upset on the radio, shore to sea, and everybody that had a marine radio heard that conversation. Trying to make light of the situation, I loaded the kids up and drove another three-plus hours to the opposite side of the state. We met in Rogers City again, only to go to sleep after our long day of travel. Fortunately, Allan was able to trade watches, and we were able to spend a few hours before Allan had to return to the boat. It was worth it in the end because we were together."

<u>A Few Great, Unusual Experiences</u>

I would have liked to have taken a trip on the ship with Allan many times, but it was difficult. Timing and logistics were so unpredictable for getting on and off the ship. I had to work, and I had nobody to watch the kids for that length of time. While aboard, when Allan was awake, he was working. And when he wasn't working, he was sleeping. It wasn't like we were on a cruise ship and our time was our own. However, I was able to take a quick trip once. I met Allan in Port Inland. His boat was out beyond the break wall, and they sent a small boat in to get me, and to drop a guy who was taking my car. He would later meet me past the locks, and I'd pick up my car and go home.

I was excited to embark on this adventure. I handed the guy the keys to my car and then we headed toward the ship, thinking this would be fun and exciting. Well, that was the case inside the break wall, but on the way out we were rocking and rolling. As we got closer to the giant ship, I felt smaller and smaller. I felt like the man in the boat in the tidy bowl commercial. The challenge was now to get from the small boat and onto the ship. That meant I had to catch a ladder rung on the side of the ship from that small boat that was rocking next to a moving ship. One wrong move, and I would be swallowed! After many attempts, I finally gripped the ladder rung, then secured a foot on the edge of the boat, trying not to lose my grip or my footing while in motion. I was successful! Once aboard, it made the journey worth it. I got to spend a little time with my husband and learn just enough to appreciate what the life of a sailor is like while on their ship."

<u>The Realities of Being a Sailor's Wife</u>

Nobody ever told us what it would be like to have a partner come and go for months on end. Maritime wives develop a routine of survival while their spouse is gone, and when our sailor husbands return, you think it's going to be much easier when they're home. We were excited for him to come home; we all missed him, but it could be difficult at times. Every time Allan came home, I wanted everything to be PERFECT. House clean, laundry is done and put away. Despite my efforts in all of that, I failed. I wasn't perfect. I was a busy, single wife and mom of two, working 40+ hours a week, and, did I mention that I am pretty unorganized; the cherry on top, I have ADD. I felt like a hamster on a wheel. Still, to this day, I swear I am the only human that can clean ALL DAY and have my house look like I did nothing. I always wanted Allan to come home to a home-cooked meal. Mealtime with two young kids in a small house could easily be overstimulating to someone who hasn't been there for a while. I didn't take into consideration the meal schedule Allan was on. So, dinner time to me was the schedule we had at home. A few times, Allan would take a few bites and then have to leave the table. I was oblivious, and he didn't say anything. I thought he didn't like my cooking.

About a year later, he asked that I not cook dinner when he first got home, He didn't want to hurt my feelings, but it was way too chaotic for him, with the loud, silly kids just being kids. It wasn't something he could adjust to that quickly.

There is also my discipline style, which is merciful and graceful. His way of discipline, cut to the quick, don't beat around the bush type of punishment, didn't always fit the crime. Often, we did not see eye to eye on this issue, and for many years, it created some conflict between us. I was the softy because I felt like I had to be both mom and dad while Allan was away. This did get easier with communication technology over time, and he became an active participant over the phone when needed. When Allan was home for a while, things started to adjust to a somewhat normal lifestyle, and then boom! Time to start thinking about him leaving again. A couple of weeks before he has to go again, the departure stress would rear its ugly head.

I will say that during the time Allan was home, he was a very active participant in our household. Cooking and cleaning, he would do anything but dust and clean toilets. He would take the kids to school, go to their school to have lunch with them, and attend every function they had while he was home. He would assist as much as he could with the sporting events. When it came to snow days, our kids HATED snow days. That meant dad made them get up and do chores; no sleeping in. Their protests and mine fell on deaf ears. They never got to do what everybody else was doing...Sleeping in! I swear the kids spent more time whining about the chores than they did to get them done. It wasn't all that bad because Allan would take them to lunch and an afternoon movie, but of course, making them get up on a snow day was cruel! How dare he!

I now often think back, wondering how the re-entry felt for Allan. It couldn't have been easy for him either. I'm sure the way we lived while he was gone was not what he thought was happening when he returned. I had my way of doing things, and he had expectations that just weren't realistic in my mind. An example of this usually happened most times when he would come home because the kids were in different stages. Certain discipline works better with a 5-year-old than it does with a toddler and vise-versa. Or things I wouldn't allow, but dad did, and vise-versa, always created some conflict and were often confusing for the kids. So yes, the cycle of re-entry was stressful. Not sure who was affected the most, but it affected all of us."

<u>Parenting Problems Can Develop</u>

The time Allan spent away from home became more difficult as the kids got older. Our Son Andrew was the rule follower, or so he made us believe (later, I learned he broke the rules but knew how not to get caught). He was a very level-headed kid, and very responsible at a young age. Looking back, I placed high expectations of him because he was so responsible and reliable. But he was just a kid, and I now feel that I had placed a burden on him that no kid should have.

Our daughter, Lauren, was always the one to push the envelope. She was our 'at risk kid.' I had her literally attached to my hip because if I didn't, God only knew the path she would have ventured on. We had to put an alarm on our home so we didn't have anyone sneaking out or sneaking in. It just wasn't going to happen on my watch. Fortunately, I was able to rely on a good friend, another Maritime wife, who was able to take our daughter and give me some respite when I needed it. There was an entire year that she wasn't left alone. I had a computer spy program so I could see what conversations were taking place on Instant Messenger and My Space. When weekend planning happened by the teenagers, I was able to see what was going to happen before it commenced. I would call my friend, and she would get Lauren for the night. I don't know what I would have done without her support! I think I'm still suffering from PTSD from their teenage years. Our daughter required a little extra help in school, which she needed but didn't want, so that was a challenge in itself. I sent this angst-struck teenage Catholic girl to a Baptist Camp, thinking that Jesus was going to make it all better. My heart was breaking for Lauren, and Allan's hands were tied. These were the times we needed him home. During this time, it was decided that I needed to be at home more than I was at work, so I reduced my full-time hours to part-time to meet the needs of our family. I swore at the beginning that I wasn't going to be that wife who would say, 'you better come home or else.' But sometimes, I regret that I hadn't. Lauren needed her dad at home.

We had the kids involved in year-round sports. Not only were they active in sports, but they were on travel teams in hockey, baseball, and volleyball. I/we became good friends with the families of other kids, so when Allan was gone, I had friends and was included because everything centered around the kids. It got to the point at one time that Allan and I only existed on paper as husband and wife because when he came home, it was "divide and conquer," taking the kids to their practices and games. At times, I was so discouraged. We were edgier with each other and had frequent disagreements. It was one of the hardest times of my life, as I know it was for Allan too. I remember Allan reassuring me that everything was going to be OK. This time will pass all too soon. This time was for the kids. We needed to keep the kids busy and with us, because of the risks we were not willing to take if we didn't keep them busy. We always knew who, what, when, and where, because they were always with us. Allan said, we will have our time, but for now, this is what we have to do.

But When the Sailor Is Home, It's Still Challenging

Again, I can really identify with these problems in Ann's story. My mother had a schedule throughout the year for school meetings, the Women's Club, church choir practice, etc. She led a single mother's life until my father came home from the ship for the winter (this was before the 60-30 contracts). My father wanted to have my mother home all the time when he was there, but my mother could not ignore the commitments she had made for the rest of the year. This created a lot of tension in our family, which eventually resulted in their divorce

The cycle continued. Until it was time for him to go again. The departure was almost as welcome as the re-entry. We were just getting used to our cycle, and then OK EVERYBODY, switch gears!!! Dad's getting ready to leave...again. So, let's try to cram all the happy times in. What is that? I didn't feel happy! We are still running around like chickens with our heads cut off, taking kids here and there, and yes, I'm still working, having to work my schedule, and home schedule, and all the rest, and now I have to take on the entertainment committee position once again. I would say to Allan for years, "Get your boat stuff ready to go so it's done, and we can just focus on us this last week." He would never do it, and I would get so frustrated and angry because the last few days, he would pack and get two months-worth of honey-dos in 3-days.

Speaking of honey-dos, I would always tell Allan, "Procrastination is the thief of time," and when he was home, to him, he had all the time in the world. I would have partly done projects that would never be completed or took years to complete. One year I gave him a long list when he first came home. Let's just say, it didn't go very well. Years later, he told me that he didn't pack for the boat ahead of time because he couldn't stand the thought of having to leave again, and the list of the unfinished honey-dos was intentional to keep his mind off having to leave. We finally came up with a good solution regarding the honey-do list. When Allan came home for 30 days, that was his time. I didn't ask him to do anything other than what was absolutely necessary or the things he wanted to do. When he came home for the winter is when he would take on the bigger projects.

Sometimes, little projects turn into bigger projects. For example, I was in our basement, and at this time, we had lived in our house for about 15 years without any evidence of mice. This time I noticed the evidence, and I freaked out. I can do almost anything, but I can't do rodents, and I have an aversion to mice! Easy to say, just set a trap, but you do not understand that I CANNOT DO IT! I mentioned this to Allan and him it was only a mouse, so no big deal. A time came and went, and by the next cold season, I was noticing a lot of evidence. I mentioned this to Allan and he said he would take care of it when he got home. I let him decompress for a few days, and then I asked him to address the situation in the basement. Weeks go by, and finally, toward the end of his time at home, Allan finally was going to take care of the pesky rodent situation. I wanted them gone for good! Allan said, 'Well, we need to call an exterminator.' When the exterminator did his assessment, he said, 'You don't have a few mice; you have families of mice.' I freaked out because Allan was going to leave in 48 hours to go back to work. It was recommended that we set traps and the exterminator would come back and set traps around the exterior of the house. I was having a meltdown because who was going to get rid of a dead mouse in a trap? Not me!

Anyway, Allan set the traps two days before his departure. The traps seemed to work almost immediately. We were sitting in our family room watching a movie, and it was like someone was making popcorn in our basement. Allan was able to take care of the majority in the first forty-eight hours. I had to set more traps after he left and then call on a neighbor to remove them. I just couldn't do it myself. Once I felt the coast was clear, I put on a mask and gloves and bleach-wiped everything down. A few years later, we had a similar situation with a bat in the attic. We only had one, but in my mind, we had a thousand!

Major Problems at Home – The Wife Must Handle Them All

I'm sure I'm not the only Maritime wife who will say this, but for me, something major would usually happen within the first few days of Allan being gone. It never failed! Basement floods, the lower-level carpet being soaked, or a leaking roof.

I also must mention that Allan came up with a bright idea to build a four-plex of condominiums. Of course, this was all going to be easy to manage from a boat! This was the plan to make some money and put our children through college debt free. The year was 2004 when it all began: property, contractors, etc. When all the units were completed, we sold two condos right away. We were then able to turn around and invest in two pieces of land in a new subdivision. We built a spec house on one parcel. Unfortunately, the economy tanked, and so did the market. We couldn't find any buyers or reliable renters with good credit, leaving us with four mortgages. It was a very stressful time. We had never intended to become landlords, it was simply something we had become by default. At a point, since many people looking for a place to buy or rent didn't have good credit, we had to take our chances. We had huge turn-overs, a few evictions, and one drug trade offense. Our tenant's sons were selling drugs out of our condo, and we had to get a lawyer, and I had to go to court for one eviction.

Some people completely trashed our places and I would have to paint, rip up the carpet and have it replaced. I remember needing to clean one of the kitchens. It was so filthy that it took me 14 hours just to clean it. The tenants hadn't lived there even for a full year, but it was so gross. I had to do what I had to do to get it ready to show, so we could get the next person in that could pay rent. In one of the homes we rented, we later found that it was used to grow Marijuana plants, which was then illegal. We attempted to sell but ended up renting for years until we were finally able to sell everything. It was such a headache because everything happened when Allan was gone. We did have a few good tenants at that time, but the majority were dirtballs. Hindsight is 20/20. What we should have done was buy a place in a college town and then rent that out while our kids went to college and have it pay for itself. Then our kids would have had a place to live.

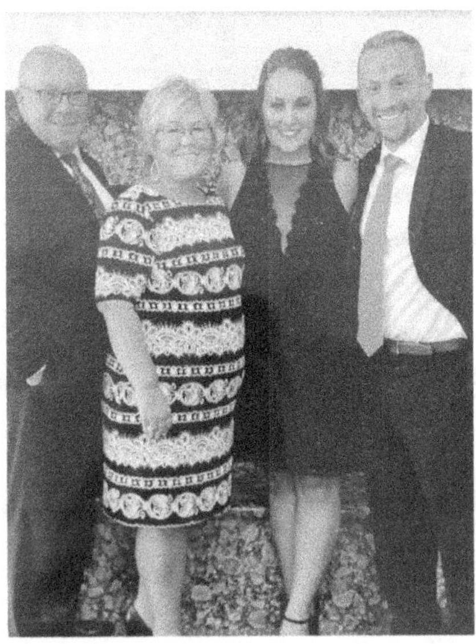

After the kids left home, I saw less and less of the families who had been a part of my life for a long time. The common denominator was gone, our kids.

That was when I started to become the 5th wheel. I didn't fit in with the married crowd, and I wasn't part of the singles crowd. Again, after all these years, I found that the evenings were lonely and the weekends lonelier. I joined a local social group on *meetup.com*.

One New Year's Eve, Allan was still out on the boat, so I joined a New Year's Eve dinner gathering with one other person I'd met previously. They happen to be one of my best friends now. The two of us had New Year's Eve dinner with eleven other strangers. After dinner, we went to a movie downtown. The movie ended just in time for the Cherry to drop at midnight. It was such a fun evening, and I have had many more outings with this group.

Summary – Was It Worth It All?

If my husband, or even my kids, were asked to tell their stories, I'm sure they would each have their own versions of the story of our lives as a maritime family. Will I do it again? I don't know, but I will say that we decided before we got into this, that we were going to be each other's strength and support. So for that reason, I can say that I am a proud wife of a Mariner. I am proud of Allan for going back to school and working very hard at the age of 31. I am proud that he wanted to provide for his family in the best way he knew how. I am proud of the sacrifices he had to make to be away from us when all he wanted to do was to be home. I am proud that he supported me and that I supported him. I became the person I am today, a very strong independent woman because of the experiences we've had as a family.

I can't compare my life to that of wives whose husbands have Monday through Friday jobs to say that it would have been much better. I only know about our life and what we accomplished together. Was it easy? Was it perfect? Hell no! But here we are, 35 years later, and I can still say that I am proud that I married a Freighter!

My story is dedicated to the maritime women of the past, present, and future. I would also like to thank my husband for everything he has done and continues to do for our family. Special thanks to the author of this book for allowing me to share some of my stories. The next chapter of my story won't be written for a few years, but I do have an idea in mind. *How do Maritime women navigate when their sailor-husbands retire?*

13

KATHY DIEDRICH

Kevin Diedrich is the Senior Chief Engineer on the Carferry 'Badger'; you can read his stories in the Sailor's Stories section below. When I was talking with Kevin, I asked if his wife, Kathy, would be willing to share her thoughts on being married to a sailor. Kevin generally spends four days aboard the Badger and is then home for four days, so the interactions with family are different from those sailing the Lakers.

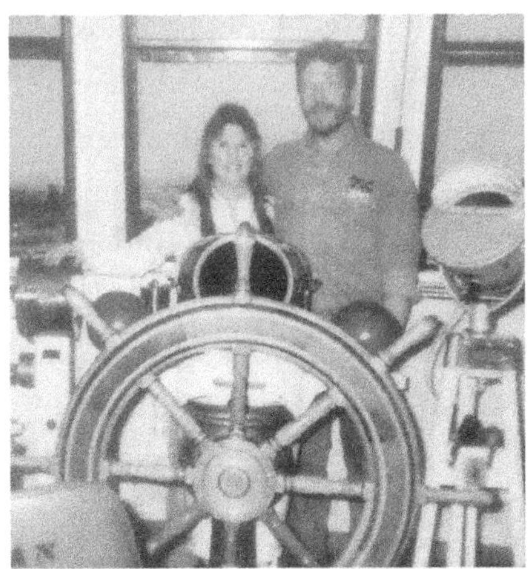

Kevin and I had been together 10 years when we FINALLY got married. A few months after getting married, Kevin applied to the United States Coast Guard to take the required exams to get his mariner's documents. I thought nothing of it until he passed his exams and received the documents that would allow him to go sailing. I remember telling him, 'We just got married, and now you're going to leave me?' He said he wanted to go back sailing because he missed it. I reluctantly agreed.

After twenty-two years of sailing, we have had our share of hardships from being separated. Kevin has been gone all summer, missing holidays, and family gatherings. I had to quickly learn how to take care of the house and the yard while working full-time.

At times, I felt like he had abandoned me to go off and have his fun on the ship. We came very close to divorce because of the hardships that come with being a Sailors wife.

Then one winter, I accompanied Kevin to the AMO (Union) school in Florida for a week. During the day, Kevin attended classes while I either lounged in the room or went outside and walked around.

During one of these walks, I came across a table with several other wives whose husbands were also attending classes. They invited me to sit with them. After introducing themselves, one of the wives asked me how long my husband had been sailing. I told her he had been sailing for about ten years, and apparently, she noticed my tone. So she asked me if I was happy with my husband's sailing. This opened up several conversations between us.

She was a remarkable person, very supportive, and easy to talk with. I will never forget how she explained the difficulties of being a sailor's wife. She explained to me how a woman must be strong to endure it. She also assured me that once you put it in perspective, the relationship can become VERY strong. She also stated that separation in a marriage can be helpful to the marriage and make it stronger because when you're reunited, there is a closer, tighter bond between you both. But she also stated that separation can destroy the marriage very quickly.

The marriages that grow stronger as a result of the husband being away at sea will never break, and it puts the sailor's wife in a unique and special category of her own, making them strong and independent. This woman made me see and realize the rewards of being married to a sailor. She showed me the inner strength I had within, one I did not even know existed. I owe this woman so very much!

In my opinion, sailors' wives are amazing! They all beat the odds for a long marriage by far. The national average is under 9 years (11 years in New York). For these kinds of marriages to thrive, there has to be a greater understanding of the challenges that will arise, even before they commit. There may be some truth to the adage, "Absence makes the heart grow fonder." Maybe the longer marriages in New York also point to the fact that challenges in a marriage make the couple work harder to succeed. The couples presented here certainly have succeeded and have done very well.

14

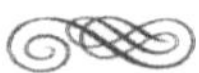

SOME SAILORS' STORIES

We haven't forgotten the men sailors. Although the first Sweet-water Sailors book concentrated on the sailors' stories, I still wanted to include some unusual stories in this sequel.

Most people who watch the ships only see the crew working out on deck, but don't think about the day-to-day life that occurs inside. Crew members have to work together and live together 24-hours per day for 60-90 days at a time, and just like "shoreside jobs", they occasionally disagree or joke around, but they still need to work safely and efficiently. The consequences of not cooperating are too serious to allow a disagreement to affect the navigation or machinery operations.

15

KEVIN DIEDRICH

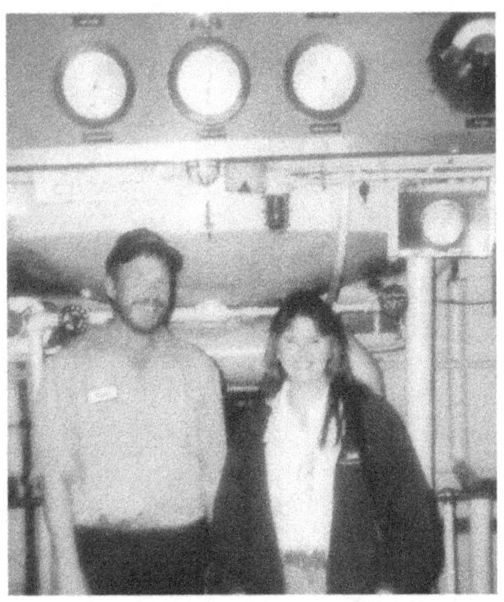

This photo was taken when Kevin was still a
Junior Engineer on the Badger.

*Since I ended the chapter on Sailors' Wives with Kathy Diedrich, I
thought it would be nice to start this section with her husband, Kevin.*

*I met Kevin Diedrich in Sturgeon Bay one winter and heard that he
worked on the Carferry "Badger," but until he became a Chief Engineer
on the Badger, I didn't get to know him well, other than the fact that he
was well-respected by many of my friends in the Great Lakes maritime*

industry. I didn't want to repeat the contributors from the first Sweetwater Sailors book, but like many people around Lake Michigan, I loved the Carferry "Badger," so Kevin was a prime candidate for the new book, because he hadn't been included in the first one.

I asked Kevin to begin with some background information, and then relate some interesting stories from his years on the Badger.

My background starts typically like that of most people who eventually come to work in the maritime business. I graduated from high school in Manitowoc, Wisconsin, and a few months after graduation, I started working at Imperial Eastman company as a Production Machinist. Three years later, I entered the United States Coast Guard (USCG), where I was stationed on the USCG 'Planetree' (WLB 307) after completing 13 weeks of basic training. The *Planetree* is a 180-foot ocean-going buoy tender, homeported in Juneau, Alaska. I served two and a half years on the *Planetree*, eventually becoming a Machinery Technician in Third Class. I then became a Second Class Machinery Technician and was transferred to the Aids to Navigation (ATON) station in Menasha, Wisconsin, where I finished my service. After my service, I went back to Imperial Eastman and was given a position in the Machine Repair Department. In 2000, I applied for and was granted my QMED document from the USCG, and in 2001 I was hired by Chief Engineer Charles Cart to work for Lake Michigan Carferry Service. I worked steadily through the QMED ranks, and then the officer ranks to my present position as Senior Chief Engineer aboard the Carferry SS "*Badger*."

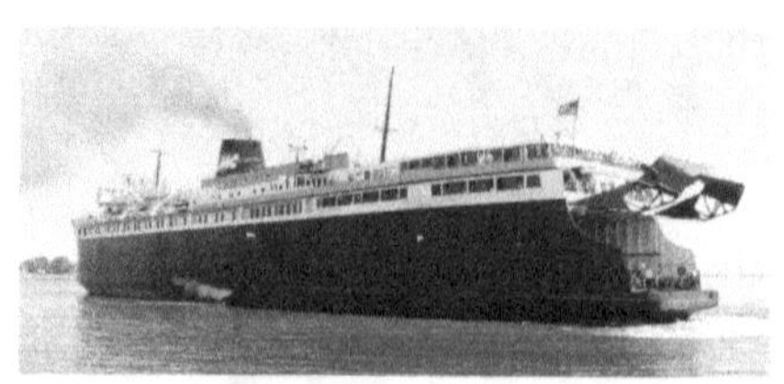

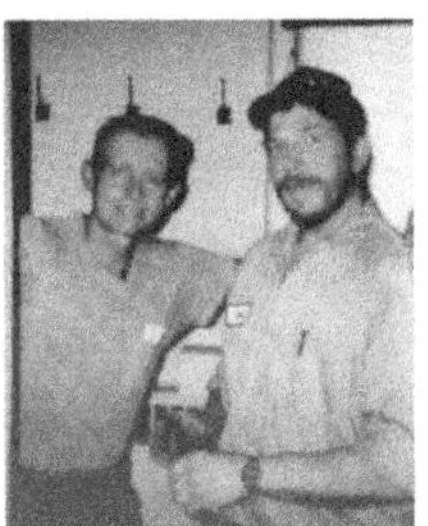

(I apologize for the poor quality of this picture, but as much as Mike and Kevin worked together, this was the only picture they could find of them together.)

Those who've read Sweetwater Sailors may recognize the name, Mike Braybrook, who also worked on the Badger, and was a major contributor of stories to that first book. The fact that Kevin and Mike worked together on the Badger, told me a lot! So, here is Kevin's story:

During my first year aboard the *Badger* as a Junior Engineer, I was working with Mike Braybrook. The Chief Engineer Cart gave me the task of installing ship lighting and emergency lighting in the newly installed Port and Starboard egress passages. I spent approximately a month and a half, 6 days a week after normal working hours, completing the installation of the fixtures and the wiring. I even made a special fixture for our press, to properly form the special wire clips we used to secure the wires.

During the US Coast Guard inspection for our COI (Certificate of Inspection), Mike and I were working in one of the after spaces, when a crew member came down and informed me that I was to report immediately to Chief Cart and the Coast Guard Inspector. The Coast Guard wanted to see me about the lighting installation in the egress passages. I confidently went up to the car deck and joined the Inspector and Chief Cart, ready to answer any questions. To my horror, the Inspector looked at me very sternly, with an unmistakable scowl, and asked me angrily if I was the person who had installed the lighting. I replied, 'Yes Ma'am.' At this point, the inspector's gaze became even angrier, and she asked in a very angry voice, 'What in the hell were you thinking when you did this project?'

I was floored! After all, Chief Cart had inspected my work after completion and said it looked great! So, at that very moment, I started to plead my case, which in reality was to throw Chief Cart under the bus. After all, I had done exactly what he instructed me to do, and he had inspected it and given me the thumbs up.

After I had pleaded my case, the Inspector lowered and shook her head. 'Damn Cheesheads,' she said. It was then that I realized I'd been set up by the Inspector and Chief Cart. To this day, it's a memory that sticks out in my mind. Working aboard a ship is no different from any other job. The only difference is that on a ship, your co-workers are more like family than anything else. Practical jokes are a common thing and crew members try and break the monotony by having a little harmless fun.

What made that first story interesting to me was that the Coast Guard Inspector was willing to be part of the practical joke. That shows me that there was an atmosphere of trust between the Badger's crew and the Coast Guard.

This next story again centers around my time as a Junior Engineer, working with Mike Braybrook. Mike and I needed some brass hardware for the ship's staterooms: hooks, eyelets, etc. We also needed ballast for a fluorescent light fixture. We had to get these items from the S.S. *Spartan*, the sister-ship of the *Badger*, which was in permanent lay-up, next to the Badger. The day before, we were to go over to the Spartan to 'harvest' the items we needed. Mike and I were talking about the movie Amityville Horror. In the movie, there is a scene where a dark, demonic, unembodied voice says, 'GET OUT'. As usual, Mike and I joked about it with each other all day.

The next morning, I went down to the Engineroom to grab my tool bag and the keys to the Spartan. I was quite early, so I decided to head over to the *Spartan* on my own to get a head start. The *Badger's* departure time was 0830. I informed the Engineer on watch that I was going over to the *Spartan* and to let Mike know that I was over there already.

Mike knew that I have a very uneasy feeling with certain parts of the *Spartan*, mainly the Cabin Deck cabins and passageways. I have no explanation for it, I just feel that I'm not alone and that I'm being watched in those areas. Well, that morning I went to the Port side passageway and started removing brass hardware. As usual, those strong, uneasy feelings started to well up inside me. Then, I started thinking about the 'GET OUT' scene from the movie and started working faster and faster, all the while being haunted by that increasing, uneasy fear.

After I had what I needed, I practically ran toward the fire safety door leading to the main lounge and sunlight, my arms full with my tool bag and the hardware. I opened up the Port fire safety door, and walked through it when suddenly, I heard a loud and menacing growl coming from the port side bar! My reaction was very much less than 'manly'. To this day, I cannot duplicate the sound of horror that came out of me. Well, as you might expect, that growl came from Mr. Braybrook, who started laughing hysterically at me and my reaction. Who can blame him? Mike had to finish harvesting what we needed as I was shaking quite a bit for quite some time afterwards."

I've been on the Spartan several times during my own inspections, and there is a very "haunted" feeling in some areas. Some of that is due to the musty, stagnant air in those closed-up rooms because I've felt that same "haunted" feeling on other old ships. It's like people are trying to talk to you from the past. I can sense Kevin's feelings in that last story.

You will notice that all three of Kevin's stories involve Mike Braybrook.

For those readers who have read Sweetwater Sailors, this may be no surprise! Many of Mike's stories in that previous book also covered very unusual circumstances. Am I starting to see a pattern here?

Here's another story about Mike Braybrook and me. We were docked in Manitowoc, WI, unloading and loading for our return to Ludington, MI. During the trip over to Manitowoc, we noticed that the Starboard propeller shaft packing was leaking, and we had run out of adjustment on the packing gland in the stuffing box. This required the addition of another ring of shaft packing. This is an arduous job as the ship was, of course, in the water with water pressure pushing inward on the shaft packing.

The space to work around the shaft packing gland is very small and tight. I was on the outboard side of the shaft and Mike was inboard of the shaft. At the time of this occurrence, I was doing a lot of reading on United States Submarines during WWII, because I had done a lot of volunteer work on the submarine, USS Cobia, and had even given tours aboard her at the Manitowoc Maritime Museum. As we backed off the packing gland, cold water started to run into the hold, pushing the existing packing out. Of course, we expected this and began installing the additional ring of packing. As I stated, this was a very difficult job to perform, and I was getting cold and frustrated.

I started to express my displeasure with the way things were going when Mike decided to motivate me by telling me just to imagine I was in a Submarine during a depth charge attack, and we were trying to stop the leak and save the Submarine. It didn't have the desired effect, as Mike had intended, and I started letting go of a very long string of expletives. Mr. Manglitz, one of the ship's owners, came into the hold right at the beginning of my expletive-laced reply to Mike. I looked up to see Mr. Manglitz looking down at me. I was, of course, very embarrassed. After we completed the job and got underway, Mr. Manglitz thanked us for our work and for getting the ship underway without delay. He then complimented me on my detailed use of the English language, and said he had never heard such a long string of colorful words flowing so effortlessly before!

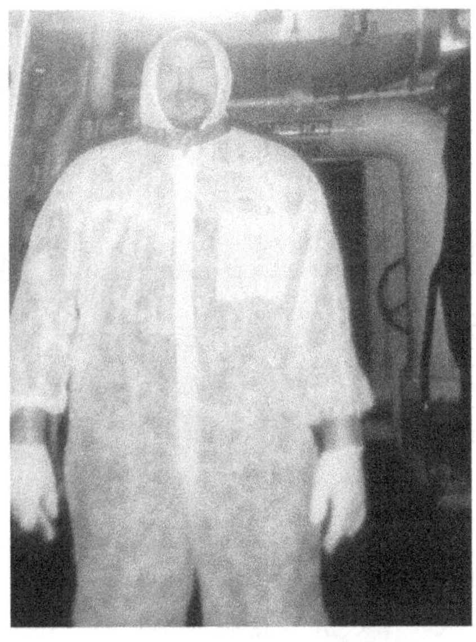

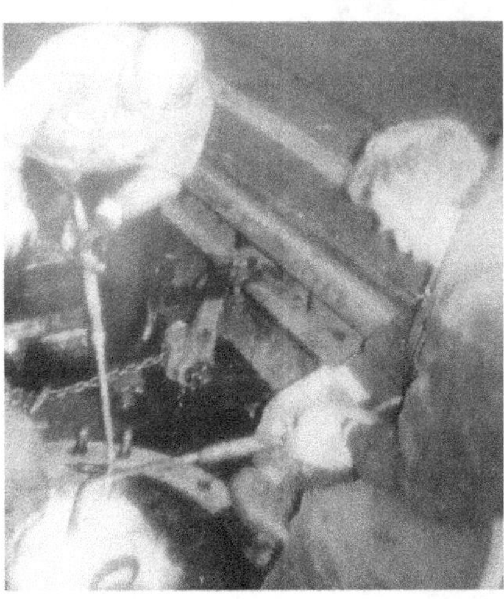

And here is one last story from the Braybrook-Diedrick escapades on the Carferry Badger:

Mike and I were working up in the cabin deck one time during the spring fit-out. The season before, I had noticed that a lighted glass sign in the starboard passageway, indicating the Women's Bathroom, did not work. I suggested to Mike that since we were ahead of schedule on our fit-out duties, we should get that light working. Mike agreed and we removed the overhead panel that would expose the wiring of the light. After the panel was removed, we noticed that the wiring had been cut at one time. This would require the installation of a Junction box and new wiring going from the Junction box to the light fixture. This was on an AC electric circuit that also operated the passageways overhead lighting to Midship.

Mike went to open the breaker to the circuit, and once he gave me the all-clear, I started to cut the old wiring out. As my knife cut through the insulation, I was given a 120-volt-AC shock that felt like someone had just taken a Baseball Bat and hit my right arm as hard as they could! Believe me, it was very painful and quite a surprise. Mike, not knowing what was happening, thought I was joking. When I informed him I was not, Mike thought I was exaggerating the pain, which I was not.

Mike then began to assure me that he had opened the breaker and killed the circuit. After a bit of back-and-forth arguing, Mike went to check the breaker. To Mike's surprise and my anger, Mike had "shut off the wrong breaker!!!" This was just another incident Mike and I would recall over the years and give each other a hard time about.

16

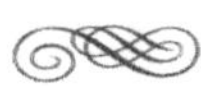

JIM COLLUM

<u>A Great Lakes Sailor With an Unusual Beginning</u>

One of the guys I've known longer than anyone on the Great Lakes is Jim Collum. A lot of people know him as "Sonny" around the Lakes. I first met him when he was an Engineer for Hannah Marine Corporation in Lemont, Illinois. Hannah had both Great Lakes tugboats as well as River towboats, and they pushed oil and asphalt barges around the Lakes, and downriver. Alexandria Barrett mentioned Jim as her Chief Engineer as part of her story in the first chapter, "Women Who Sail the Great Lakes."

Jim has a well-rounded career, both on Great Lakes tugboats and on Lakers (cargo ships), but I wasn't aware of how he started, and then ended up with Hannah Marine, where I first met him. When I asked him to document his story for this sequel, his first memories were river-related, not Lakes-related, but it all comes together, and I think you'll love Jim's story.

<u>Small World</u>

My first job on a river boat came in the summer of 1978. There were 26 Towboat/Barge Line Companies in Greenville Mississippi at the time, and I applied at about half of them in one day. I had checked into the old Downtowner on First Street and planned to stay until I got a job. Early that evening, I got a call from Wilkerson Barge lines for a deckhand job on the M/V *Judy C.*

A plane ride later, I was in St. Louis heading out to catch the boat at Lock 26. I thought that was a strange name for a town, but I told the cab driver, and he seemed to know where to go. You see, I had never been on or even seen a true towboat and had no idea what a "lock" was (a large chamber for lowering and raising vessels on rivers and canals).

We arrived at lock 26 and pulled right up to the edge of the lock. I asked the cab driver why we stopped there, and he said, "this is Lock 26!" I asked him where the boat might be, and he said it was most likely in the lock! Well, I took a look down into the lock, and sure enough, the *Judy C.* was there. An older gentleman manning a large nylon line saw me and waved me down. You have to understand that this was back when there was no fence around facilities of this kind, no security, and access was completely open. So, I grabbed my Samsonite and headed down the ladder to the stern of the barge.

The gentleman manning the stern line turned out to be the Chief Engineer, George Nail, filling in as a deckhand because the crew was one short (I was the new deckhand). He asked me a few questions about experience and quickly found that I had none, so he stayed at his post and began to train me on what the job entailed. It wasn't long before he asked me my name. "Jim Collum," I said. Then he asked me where I was from, and I said I was from Tomnolen, Mississippi! He broke out in a wide grin and asked me, "Is your dad Carl Collum?" I told him yes, that is my dad. His smile got even broader, and he said, "I used to buy Whiskey from your dad when I was young!"

George Nail and Earnest Eans were the two Chiefs on the *Judy C.* when I started. They were 58 and 65 years old, respectively. They were my ticket to the engine room and two of the best teachers I have ever known. I guess my dad sold Whiskey to the right guy!

In the Autumn of 1979, I was working on the Judy C. on the Illinois River for Wilkerson Barge Lines. We had two brand new black oil barges, just built by St. Louis Ship, the JPW-1 and JPW-2. Hannah Marine had chartered the tow boat and both of the new barges to work the asphalt trade in the Chicago/Indiana Harbor area.

Things were going fairly well until late one night, I awoke from a sound sleep to the sound of metal scraping and crushing noises. I ran out of my room, in nothing but my 'fruit of the looms', coming out onto the side deck just in time to see the Wheelhouse getting crushed under the B & O Railroad bridge, just South of the Trumbull asphalt dock.

Our pilot (a rather large man) was crawling out of a small wheelhouse window screaming, 'Tell the Chief to back her down,' as we were still moving forward, with no control. Mr. Earnest, our Chief, had just come out on deck, and he said, 'Back her down with what?' There were no other engine controls except those in the pilothouse! The Judy C. had a retractable wheelhouse, and the Pilot had not lowered it enough to clear the B & O railroad bridge, which caused our accident. That accident sent the tow boat off to the shipyard for repairs!

We were still under charter with Hannah but had no vessel to move the barges, so Hannah took over with their local tugs to do the job. The crew of the Judy C was still responsible for Tankerman services on the two barges, however! Because I had a Tankerman endorsement and was the only one with a driver's license and a credit card, the company asked me to get a rental car and follow the barges around the south end of Lake Michigan, loading and unloading them.

Hertz let me have a white 1979 T-Bird with a light blue interior. I kept it for over a month, going dock to dock, loading and unloading the two JPW Barges. Now, when you load and unload Asphalt barges, you tend to get some of the product on your hands, clothes, shoes, and most all other exposed body parts. This doesn't look good on the baby blue upholstery of a brand-new T-bird.

I slept in the T-bird when possible and sometimes even napped in the warm Boiler Room of one of the barges. Now and then, I made it back to Lemont Ship, where the Judy C. was undergoing repairs, and I'd catch up on some much-needed sleep!

Meals were either a fast-food sandwich or one of the Hannah tug crew would invite me to dine with them. It was here that I was told that Hannah Marine was in search of an engineer, and when I found out the pay scale, I knew that I was their man! I went in for an interview and got the job, but I told personnel that I had to give two-weeks notice to Wilkerson Barge line. I had two weeks left on my hitch on the Judy C., and after about a month and a half, the Judi C was repaired and underway again. On the last day of my hitch, we were approaching the Hannah Marine Shipyard and headquarters in Lemont, and I went up to the wheelhouse and told Slim, our Pilot, to pull the boat over because I was getting off! Slim said, "You can't get off." I informed him that I was quitting and that I needed him to get close to the dock. Slim slowly nudged the barge next to Hannah's dock wall, and I got off to start my new job. That was the 18th of December, 1979. I stayed there for 29 years!"

I can identify with this next story by Jim Collum because I am also very prone to motion sickness. I have taken pills on most of my ship-riding jobs before leaving the dock, just to be on the safe side, but the two worst sea-sickness episodes in my career were aboard tugboats, one on

Lake Michigan, and the other was a Hannah Marine tug heading from Fort Lauderdale to Baltimore. I wanted to die, and it is very embarrassing when you are with a seasoned crew who do not get sick.

So, here is Jim's story about being a Seasick Sailor.

My first trip with Hannah Marine was on the Donald C. Hannah, on a run to Ludington, Michigan, for a barge load of Calcium Chloride coming out of the Dow Chemical plant. Calcium Chloride is a salt brine of around 35% or more, used in dust control on roadways, ice and snow melting, and in food processing. The Plant is now owned by Occidental Chemical Company, but they still make the same products today, coming out of Ludington, and have been doing so since 1942.

Now, with this being my first trip on water other than a river, I was not ready for a December Gale in Lake Michigan. I not only thought I was going to die, but I wanted to die! I don't pray much, but I prayed for land that night! I didn't even know what seasickness was until that night out on Lake Michigan. It was only about an 18-hour run, but on the Donald C. Hannah, it was like a cork in a bathtub! You see, the Donald was only 90 feet long. It was tender in any sea over 4 feet.

When we got to Ludington, my prayers had been answered, and I felt like a million Dollars. There was a phone for the boat crew to use in the water intake house at the dock, so off I went to find an airport to take me away from this nightmare. Much to my dismay, the nearest Airport was in Muskegon, 58 miles south, and I had no way of getting there. Captain Gary Schmidt talked me into staying on board for the trip back to Chicago, and, as fate would have it, Lake Michigan was as flat as a mirror on the trip back. "This ain't so bad," I thought..." maybe I'll stay around a little longer!"

Stay around I did, but seasickness has no cure, only medicines like Bonine and Dramamine. They ease nausea, but they also put you to sleep! One newer medication, Transderm Scopolamine, comes in the form of a patch, about the size of a dime, that you stick behind your lower ear, and its effects are good for several days. If you need continued medication, then you put a new patch behind the opposite ear. On the Great Lakes, I only used them occasionally, but on the open ocean, I often wore them for a whole 30-day hitch.

In my 29 years at Hannah Marine, there were maybe five sailors I worked with who did not get sick at some point. I remember we would get guys from the freighters who had sailed for years. "I don't get seasick," they would say, only to get sick. A tug boat is a little different from a 600-foot or more ship.

People who are not familiar with the Great Lakes may think that they are calm compared to the ocean, but the truth is that the storms on the Great Lakes are "just plain different." The period of the seas (distance between waves) is much shorter than the ocean, which doesn't give the ship a chance to recover before the next wave hits. The following story from Jim Collum helps to describe what happens in a Great Lakes storm.

Band-Aids on the Hull

It was late in the shipping season on the McKee Sons, and the Gales of November were in full force. The McKee Sons was built in 1945 as a Troop Transport vessel and Christened "Marine Angel." (If you want a good read, *Until the Sea Shall Free Them*, is the story of the Marine Electric) After the war, the vessel was sold to the Marine Coal Company and used as a Coal carrier until it was sold to the McKee Family and converted to a self-unloading bulker in 1953.

The ship operated until it was laid up, from 1980 until 1990. It was then converted into a barge with a notch for an articulated tug to push it. However, the pilothouse and deck crew quarters remained forward, with the engineers living on the tug. There was also a galley and crew's mess aft, in the starboard notch of the barge. The pilothouse controls for the engines and steering on the tug were connected by an 'umbilical cord'. All of these things made this articulated arrangement very unusual.

The Tug Invincible had a 'Bludworth' ATB (Articulated Tug Barge) system in use, and it pushed the McKee Sons from 2001 until December 2012.

Late in the afternoon in question, we had passed The Mackinac bridge, and the weather was rapidly deteriorating. Sometime around 2100 hours, when we had passed Lansing Shoals, I went forward to check with Captain Tom Bell on our weather route plans. Captain Bell said confidently, "we're going into Green Bay through Deaths Door. I think we can make it." He said this even though the seas were getting worse. I headed aft alongside AB Dan Manning (now Captain Manning). As we made our way down the Starboard side of the old McKee, the waves were rolling down the deck so badly that Dan and I had to keep each other from being washed overboard.

In all my years on the Great Lakes, this was the first time I'd witnessed breakers rolling down the main deck! ......*Freeboard???....Not enough for these Seas!!!* ....We made it aft, but not before the waves had destroyed a large, portable diesel heater and one of our fuel station containment pans (installed beneath fueling stations to catch any spilled fuel).

Once aft, I made my way back onto the tug, where all of the Engineering crew were berthed on the Invincible. Scotty Chouinard was the Engineer on watch, and I let him know what Captain Bell's plan was. He seemed a bit skittish, but we both agreed that there wasn't much we could do except hang on. I went to bed and somehow managed to sleep through most of the night. The banging woke me up, and a couple of times, it threw me against the bulkhead or almost out of bed.

When I finally did get up, we had already anchored in Manitowoc, and the Seas had calmed down to almost nothing. I dressed and went forward to the tug's galley, and there was Scotty with a pile of cigarette butts in the ashtray and candy wrappers all over the table. He immediately cried out, "I don't know what broke, Chief, but something broke"

"I'm sure we'll find it," I said.

Well, it didn't take long. I told Scotty to join me for breakfast (our galley was on the aft starboard wing, part of the old ship). For access to the barge from the tug, we used the port hatch on the second deck of the tug. When I opened this hatch, suddenly, I could see the sun shining through a huge fracture inside the notch of the barge. "Hey, Scotty. Here's what you heard break last night!" I told him.

We went up the gangway to the barge and saw the rest of the damage. The crack ran almost across the port deck of the notch. This is a 1¼" steel plate, and the fracture was about 15 feet long! I told Scotty that I was going forward to get Captain Bell, as I didn't want to break news like this over the radio. Our Pumpman, Steve Grulke, was having a smoke on the deck and asked me what was wrong. I pointed to the fracture and headed forward. After briefing Captain Bell on our issue, we both came back aft to inspect the damage. We arrived to find that someone (Pumpman???) had put Band-Aids from our medical kit all along the crack!!! I didn't know what to say, and I could see that Captain Bell was not happy.

A temporary repair was authorized by the Coast Guard, and Scotty and the other Assistant Engineer, Ken Siford Jr., welded some patches across the crack. We were then allowed to proceed to Milwaukee for permanent repairs. This took several days, as there was a great deal of framing damage to the internals of the notch wing walls.

The McKee Sons only sailed for one more year after that. We laid her up on Christmas Eve of 2012. It sat for a couple of years in Erie, PA, and is now laid up in Muskegon, Michigan.

Another one from Jim, emphasizing the hard work required to run some of the "ancient" equipment found on the Great Lakes.

Engines for a Match

The Tug James A Hannah was well-known on the Great lakes for many years. It was a unique vessel built in 1943 as an Army LT (large tug). In 1967 Cristy Corporation (now Fincantieri Sturgeon Bay) did the repower conversion from steam to Diesel, installing two Fairbanks Morse, 38D 8-1/8, direct reversing 10-cylinder OP's (Opposed Piston) engines, giving the tug about 3,600 Horsepower. This was under the ownership of Bultema Dock and Dredge Company out of Muskegon, Michigan. Hannah Marine later purchased the tug in 1973 and named it after the family patriarch.

Not only were the engines direct reversing, but they were coupled to a Lufkin Compound Reduction Gear driving only one propellor. This being the case, two operating modes were available —Master and Slip.

In the Master Mode, both engines were cranked either ahead or astern, and the clutches were already engaged. So, with an 11' wheel, the tug would jump 50 feet if you started both engines in Master ahead or astern. Engine speed could be brought up, but to stop the wheel, you had to stop the engines.

In 'slip' mode, the starboard engine was started in 'ahead', and the port engine was in reverse. The slip control was then actuated either ahead or astern, and the engine called for would engage that clutch, move the controller ahead, and get the starboard engine and the wheel turns for forward movement. If you move the slip controller aft, you would get the port engine for aft movement. This slip mode was used for most maneuvering in tight quarters or rivers. There was a shaft brake on the output tail shaft, so in either mode, the brake would apply (through air controls), and the wheel would stop.

The master mode was used primarily underway or when both engines were needed for reverse power. Now the *James A Hannah* had a few years of wear on it when in 1981, we were breaking ice in the Straits of Mackinaw. This was a particularly bad year for ice, and the straits were packed. The age of the equipment and wear on the controls came into play in situations like this, and instead of the captain starting and stopping the engines from the wheelhouse, the engineer had to manually do this in the engine room, on the old WABCO (Westinghouse Air Brake Company) units. One of the reasons for this was that every start from the Wheelhouse required a greater amount of air, and this would lead to a loss of air pressure after about 6 starts, regardless of direction. The other reason was that the captain (or Mate) would fail to notice that the engines had started and kept expelling the compressed air.

Now you must understand that the James A Hannah had 120 air valves for main engine control, and all of them had to work for the shifting maneuvers to go right. So, in ice-breaking situations, it was best practice for the Engineer to start and stop the engines from the engine room, actually using the controllers mounted on the side of each engine, in such positions that the Engineer could grab the handles and start them both either ahead or astern. They both had to be started together due to the compound reduction gear in place and the clutches engaged in Master Control.

When the captain wanted Master Control, he would call down on the sound-powered phone and let me know. In Master, I would watch the WABCO Controllers mounted on the sides of the engines. If a signal from the Wheel house caused them to shift slightly ahead, then I would crank them in Ahead. And if after a stop they might shift slightly Astern, I would crank them for astern. It was a tedious, boring job that required a lot of arm strength.

On this particular trip, breaking ice in the straits, I had been down below cranking engines for about 6 hours, and at the time, I was a heavy smoker. I ran out of matches and needed a smoke, so I called Captain Hebert and asked him to send someone down with matches or a lighter. He agreed. Thirty minutes went by, and no matches. Another thirty minutes, and still no matches. Captain

Nutsie Hebert (pronounced Newtsee Abear) was well known on the Great Lakes and was a legend at Hannah Marine. He also had a short fuse but was one of those guys that got over it real quick (thankfully).

After more than an hour passed without receiving my matches, I got the signal for Master Ahead, but I didn't start the engines. In less than 15 seconds, I got a call from Captain Nutsie, screaming at me, wanting to know why the engines weren't started, "What's Da matter with you Chief? Start the GD Engines!" I told him I needed matches to start the engines!!! He got even madder, but my point was made.

I started the engines, but not before I got my matches!!! Captain Nutsie got over it, eventually!

(This summer will make 44 years Sailing for Jim Collum. Most of it was on the Great Lakes, and 41 of those as Chief Engineer!)

17

SHAUN VARY

I met Shaun through the Internet during my search for Great Lakes Commercial Fishermen, while doing research for another book. Although Shaun is not a fisherman, he comes from seven generations of Canadian commercial fishermen on Lakes Huron and Erie. He is actually a Great Lakes sailor. Shaun does his best to keep the history of all the Canadian Lake Erie-style fish tugs alive and has self-published a couple of books on fish tugs (Google "Shaun Vary Collection" to see his photos). Shaun has a lot of friends who are fishermen, and he put me in touch with many of them.

Shaun's sailing career started in 1987 when he attended Georgian College in Owen Sound, Ontario. After graduating, he took a shore job with Ontario Hydro, because it was near impossible to get a job aboard a ship at the time. Shaun worked ashore for about 9 years before going back to sailing. He has worked for Algoma, Canada Steamship Lines, Lower Lakes Towing (twice), and Mckeil Marine (twice). He is now starting his 15th season as Chief Engineer in the 2022 season.

Shaun builds ship models; I saw one while visiting with Ed Wiltse, because Ed and Shaun worked together at one time. He also has a retired fishing tug (pictured here) that he is rebuilding in his spare time. She's a real beauty and very representative of the older Great Lakes fish tug style. In addition to building ship models and rebuilding fishing tugs, Shaun also builds models of tugs and Great Lakes freighters. In his younger days, he dabbled in many other things, even using discarded cigarette packages and scotch tape as early crude materials to build waterline models of Lake Erie-style tugs, which he and his brother played with on their carpeted floor, along with Lego-built harbors and fishing shanties.

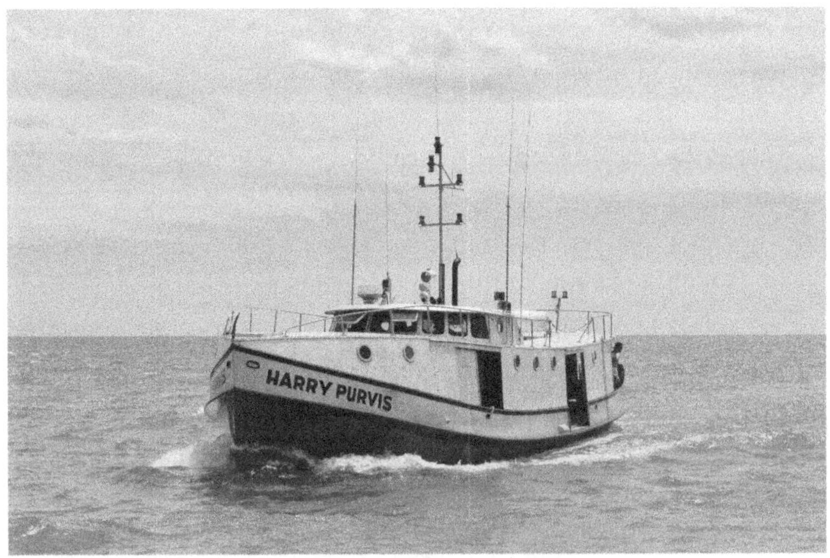

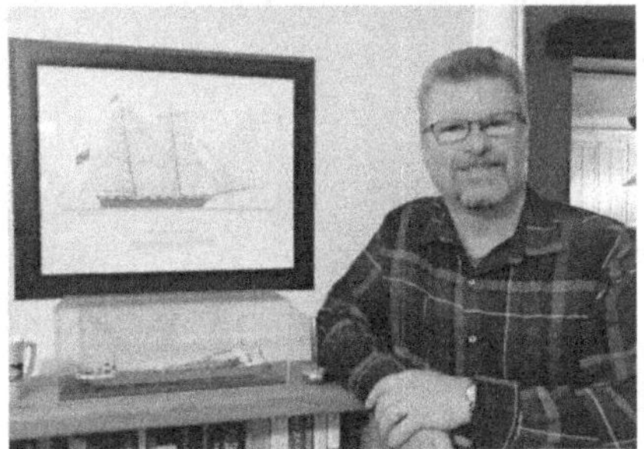

Captain Ed Wiltse with one of Shaun Vary's
ship models.

The following are some of Shaun's sailing stories:

Cooks/Food

I have sailed with several galley crews over the years. Some were chefs, some were cooks, and some couldn't 'vittle' a woodpecker in Sherwood Forrest. When you are stuck on a freighter during a holiday, a good dinner can make a huge difference in morale. The companies used to send lots of extra goodies to make Christmas or Thanksgiving dinners even more special. Unfortunately, this is not a trend that has continued.

One cook that I sailed with for many years would make 'low-fat' macaroni and cheese. The crew enjoyed it, but there was nothing 'low-fat' about it! The first ingredient was a 5-pound brick of yellow cheese. One time, while sailing across Lake Superior, the cook made pizza for lunch, which is always a favorite. A new deckhand wanted to know how we were able to get pizza delivered way out in the middle of the lake. He refused to believe that the cook had made the pizza on board. We all had a good laugh at that one.

Often, during winter work, the engineers had to fend for themselves in the galley. It can be hard to resist using the deep fryer every day, but necessary to keep the arteries clear. One year, my brother and I were on board working together while dry-docked at Sturgeon Bay. We had been enjoying one of the local delicacies - deep-fried cheese curds - at various restaurants in the area. We thought it would be a good idea to try to make them ourselves on board. The first step was finding some cheese curds on Christmas Eve. We were out getting some supplies and asked the friendly gentleman at one of the stores if there was a spot where we could get some cheese curds. He replied, "Well, you can get them at Wal-Mart, but they won't be squeaky!" My brother and I still chuckle at that one whenever the topic of cheese curds comes up. By the way, our deep-fried cheese curd experiment didn't exactly turn out, but it still tasted good.

<u>Cadet Time:</u>

Many moons ago, I was a cadet aboard the Algosoo (ii). It was my first time working on board a lake freighter, although I had been exposed to them from a young age. I took in the experience and was made to feel like a valuable member of the engine room crew. One memory of that time that still sticks out in my mind, is a day that we were in port doing some repairs to the port main engine. The Second Engineer (First Assistant Engineer on American vessels) and his Machinery Assistant had to replace a leaking exhaust bellows on top of the engine. The bolts holding it in place had to be burned off with a cutting torch, and I was assigned to the duty of 'fire watch'. This meant that I was positioned between the two engines, with a dry chemical fire extinguisher, and was given specific instructions to put out any serious fires.

After a few minutes of sparks flying everywhere, a coco mat erupted into flames on the catwalk between the two engines. I leaped into action, pulling the pin and dousing the fire with the dry chem unit I had been put in charge of. Just as my training had taught me! The fire was out! A few seconds later, the cloud of dry chem powder cleared, and I was greeted by the sight of the Engineer and M/A kneeling on top of the engine, completely covered in white powder. They were not amused, but after a few minutes of colorful language, we were all laughing about it. I couldn't be scolded for doing exactly what I was told to do.

Another incident I remember, happened one beautiful summer day while downbound in lower Lake Huron. I was the second engineer aboard another laker now gone for scrap. I was out on deck enjoying the sunshine before I had to get ready to go on watch. Three deckhands had assembled aft to re-spool the wire onto the port aft mooring winch. The 1st mate instructed them to let the wire go out of the fairlead and down into the water to get the nasty *'dog's nest'* of the spooled wire off of the winch drum and then spool it back on nice and neat. I happened along just as the wire that had been laid down into the lake was suddenly pulled tight, and all of the remaining wire on the drum rapidly spooled off into the lake with it. One of the guys said to me, 'It's like something down there pulled it off!'

As my brain was registering what had just happened, I quipped,

'Now what down there would pull that off?' about the same time that I bolted toward the engine room. Sure enough, a large jolt had gone through the power plant, and our speed suddenly dropped off. I arrived in the engine control room just in time to answer the Captain's phone query as to what was going on. We had to stop in Sarnia and send divers down to look at our propeller. Most of the winch wire was neatly wrapped around it. Luckily, no damage had been done. Those deckhands received some good hands-on experience that day, and one of them is now a captain.

The G.P.'s New Pants:

You sail with many interesting crewmates over the years, and after spending a lot of time with the same guys, they become like family. Conversely, you can get stuck working with people you don't necessarily get along with. It still takes teamwork to make the ship run smoothly, day-in and day-out.

I sailed with one fellow over the years who was a reliable crewman, team player, and good shipmate. He was like family when aboard. One of his quirks was that he did not like to buy new work gear. He had a knack for finding 'used but good' items that he would thrift for himself. He could be found working in coveralls that were way too large for him, or a pair of work boots with each boot being different styles and sizes. He was working in the tunnel on board the self-unloader we were assigned to, and during one of his times off, he broke down and decided to buy a brand-new rain suit to wear when hosing. He took a good ribbing from the crew for actually having to purchase something new to wear to work.

Just after returning to work with his new waterproof jacket and pants, we were 'fortunate' to get a load of furnace flue dust from one of the steel mills in Hamilton, going to Burns Harbor. It was loaded in the pouring rain and took several hours to get on board. After a day's sail, the head conveyorman decided to open some of the unloading gates in the tunnel and see how the cargo would flow onto the belt. Nothing came down through the gates from the full cargo holds above. The wet, powdery cargo had turned into a non-free-flowing mass in the cargo holds. We knew that the unload was not going to go well.

After a day of trying to get any amount of unloading rate at Burns Harbor, it became evident that help would be needed to get the cargo out of the ship. Eventually, workers were brought in to go inside the cargo holds with air lances to break up the cargo, and a long-armed backhoe was positioned on shore to help push the cargo down onto the gates. This way, the ship's unloading system could be used to get the cargo on shore for the customer. One drawback was that the unloading system belt pulleys on the ship would get buried with cargo after a few hours of unloading, and we would have to shut down to clean up.

As a time-saving measure, vacuum trucks were brought in to suck the spilled cargo away from the pulleys. These were powerful trucks with 6-inch suction hoses. My above-mentioned tunnel man friend was on hand for the trial run with the first vacuum truck, and he was wearing his brand-new raincoat and rain pants. The ship's wash-down hoses could be used to help push the sticky cargo toward the vacuum truck's suction hose, hence the rain suit. There was an operator from the truck running the hose at the suction pipe, and he was in radio contact with another operator at the truck.

The tunnel man stood by beside the man with the suction hose. The order was given to start up the truck's suction pump. Suction could be heard building in the truck's hose. It went to full suction, and the operator began moving the end of the hose around to collect the cargo. He moved the hose toward the man in the brand new bright yellow rain suit. Like something out of a Saturday morning cartoon, the rain pants were ripped off and sucked up the truck's hose in a flash. The result was a sad and slightly unnerved expression from one man, surrounded by hoots of laughter from everyone else! I think his next pair of rain pants were 'used but good'.

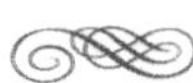

18

BOB HAWORTH

I'm ending this section with Bob Haworth because he is a full-time sailor, but also an unusual one, leading into the next chapters of this book. And I mean "unusual" in a very complimentary way!

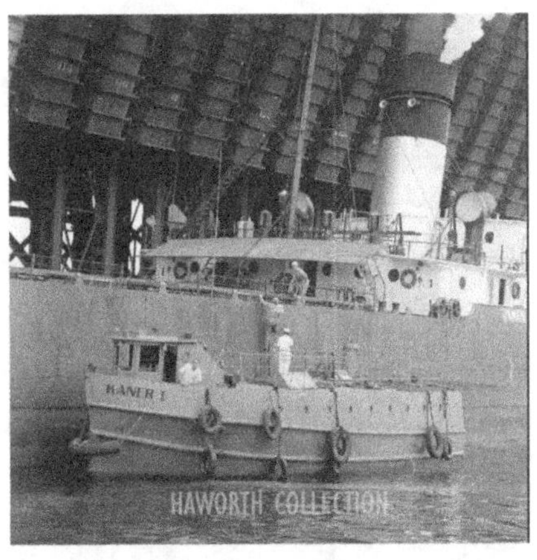

I found Bob Haworth late in my preparation of the original Sweetwater

Sailors book. I had a chapter on unusual ships in that book and one of the subjects was Bum Boats. I didn't have any good pictures of Bum Boats and I bumped into one on Facebook, posted by Bob Haworth. I asked for permission to use that picture in Sweetwater Sailors, but I also 'friended' Bob on Facebook. I have been impressed by his posts ever since, and I knew I wanted him in this sequel

Bob is a great photographer, both color and black & white. He intends to publish his own book one of these days.

But I have also been impressed by the thoughtfulness in his posts, including his memorials to celebrities who pass away, particularly musicians whose music has affected Bob's life, such as when John Prine died. I then started seeing photos of Bob playing guitar, and one with him playing the saxophone, so I asked Bob how many instruments he played. "I can't think of very many that I can't play," was his response.

So, you see, Bob is a 'multi-dimensional' Great Lakes sailor, and I know that you will enjoy the following story and photographs that Bob graciously provided for this book.

The following is in Bob Haworth's words.

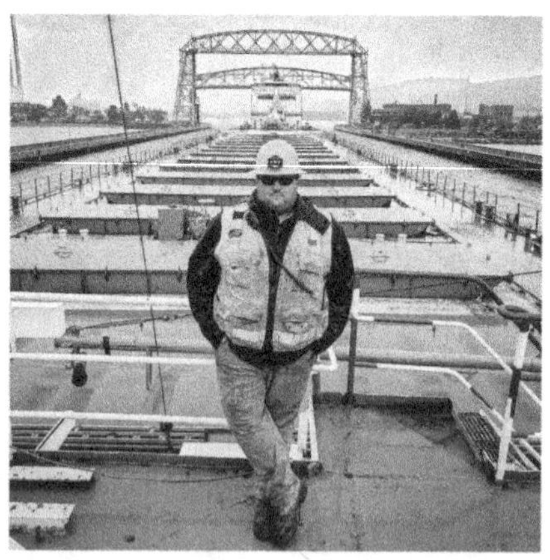

I remember thinking of how cool it would be to be aboard, and all the places I could see that I'd only read about in books. It was on that day that I knew what I wanted to do with my life. How does a young kid know at that age? I have no idea, honestly. It was just one if those things you know. You don't know why, but you just know.

I had already known about the boats on the lakes by then, but I hadn't had any thoughts about working on them. Well, none that were serious anyhow. I grew up in Lewiston, a small town in Northern Lower Michigan, an hour or more drive to any large body of water. There weren't many sailors from my area; most of them were an hour away in Rogers City and Alpena. It was the result of a 4th grade Michigan History project on the Soo Locks and the Edmund Fitzgerald that really planted the seed in my interest in the Lake boats. My teacher's dad was Captain on the Arthur M. Anderson. That following summer, my friend and our mothers were treated to a tour aboard the Anderson while she loaded at Calcite.

In years to follow, my interest in the shipping industry gradually grew, but in equal proportion to my interest in its history as well. My family's summer vacations always consisted of visiting at least one museum on the lakes. For one week a summer, sometimes two, we would camp in the Soo, and that is where I got to meet up with other people who had similar interests. It was a great way to grow up, and I wouldn't trade it for anything. I spent my off time when I was younger, with my nose buried in books about the Lakes and the lake boats. I wanted to know everything I could.

To this day, I'm still heavily involved with the preservation of maritime history on the Lakes, even with a full-time career in their waters. For the last few years, I've been on the board of the Marine Historical Society of Detroit, an organization of Great Lakes Historians dedicated to the preservation of Maritime History on the Great Lakes.

Lots of earth and water have passed beneath me since then, and somewhere along the way, I lost touch with the young man that knew what he wanted his future to hold for him that day, some 720 feet above Lake Superior, high atop Brockway Mountain. I did, however, fulfill that dream to 'sign the articles' for the greatest adventure of my life, and I got to see all those ports I had read and heard about.

I've worked every unlicensed job there is aboard a boat. Wiper, Gateman, 2nd Cook, OS, AB, AB Wheelsman, and AB Maintenance Man. I wouldn't trade it for anything. It suits me, and I suit it. No day out here is the same. To be part of a great team out here is a great feeling. Every year we make 50-60 trips, safely and professionally.

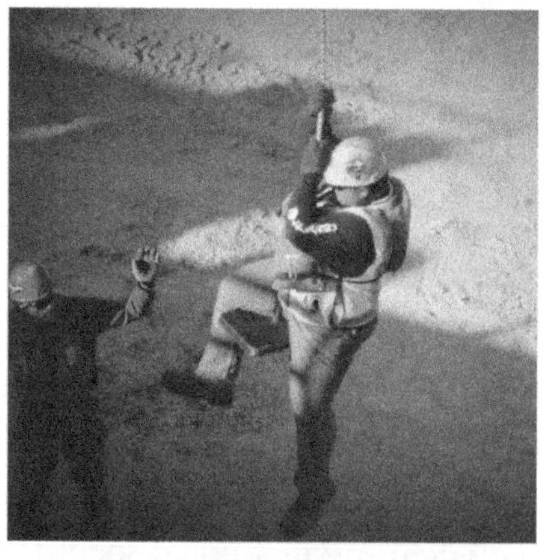

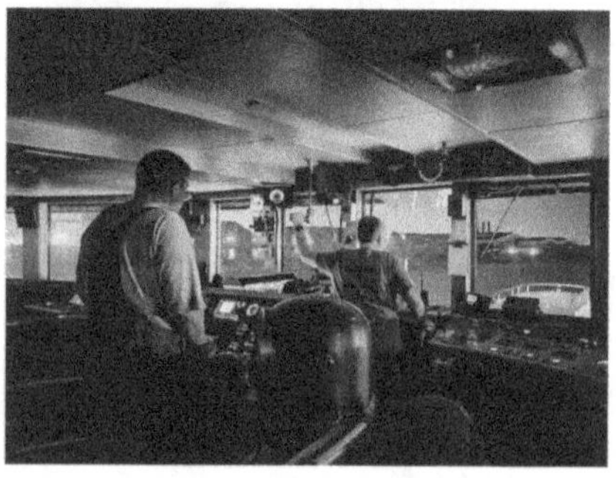

On average, I spend about 155 days or more out here each year. Yes, that is a long time to be away from home. However, I don't have anything holding me at home right now, so that does make it a little bit easier. What doesn't get easier, though, is saying goodbye when it's time to leave. I do have a lot to keep me busy out here, though. One of my favorite past times is music.

When I was a kid, my parents had an extensive music library that I would browse through quite frequently. I remember listening to radio shows on shortwave stations late at night in the summer when the conditions allowed. It was as if I could travel anywhere in the world, without leaving my house. I learned a lot about different places by listening to the radio. I learned a lot about life also, from listening to the story that each song conveyed. As I got older, I started focusing on instrumentation rather than lyrics, and I picked up the guitar.

I've been playing since age five. Country, Rock, Folk, Americana, Bluegrass... I love it all. I also love Jazz and Dixieland (New Orleans Jazz), and I played Saxophone in the high school Jazz Band, as well as the concert band. In all, I can play, but never mastered, twelve instruments. But out of all of them, I prefer my guitar.

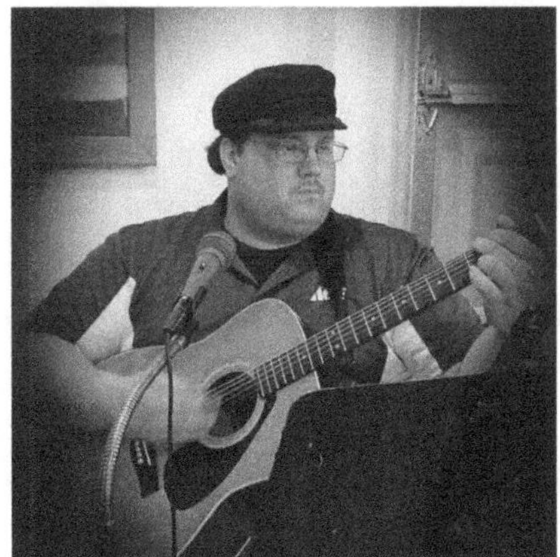

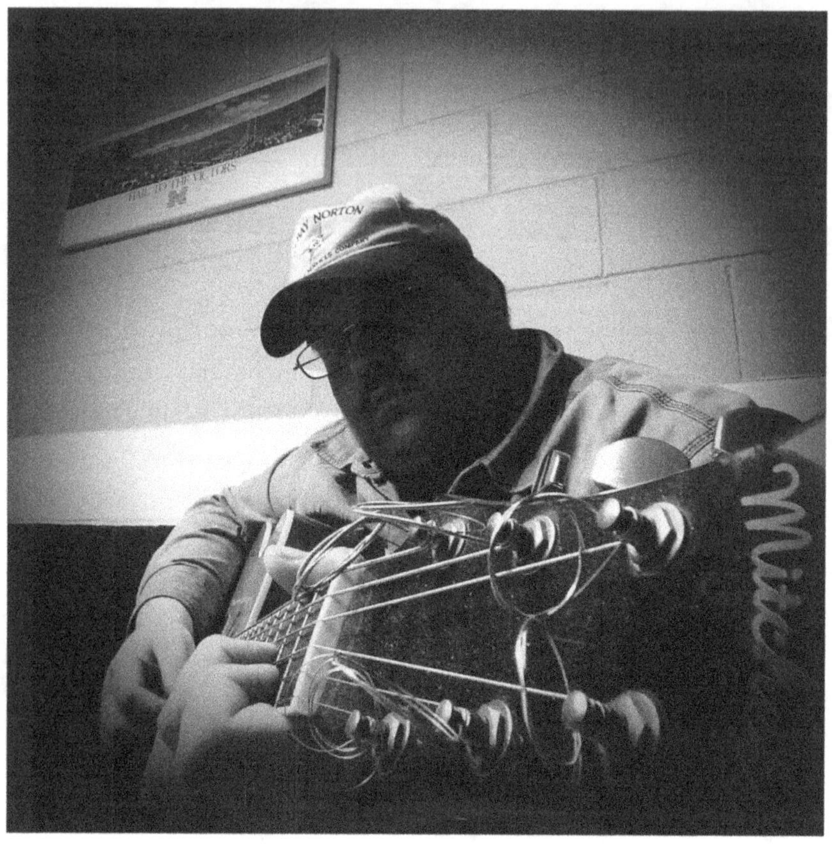

My Martin has traveled with me many a mile and has been aboard every boat I've been on. It's quite fun sometimes, especially when other crew members who are musically inclined bring their instruments out, and we blow off some steam with an impromptu jam session. We sing, critique each other, but we also help each other as musicians. I've made many friends ashore and on the water through music. Life is a song, and I play it every chance I get!

So, that's me in a nutshell. Able seaman, lover of music, musician, artist, traveler, and explorer of life. I'm not sure how long I will continue my career out here. I treat each day like it were the last. That way, when the last day does come, I can say that I did it and did it whole-heartedly, the right way, the first time. One day I'll hang it up, but until then, I'll keep steamin' and steering. Headed for wherever the compass rose takes me.

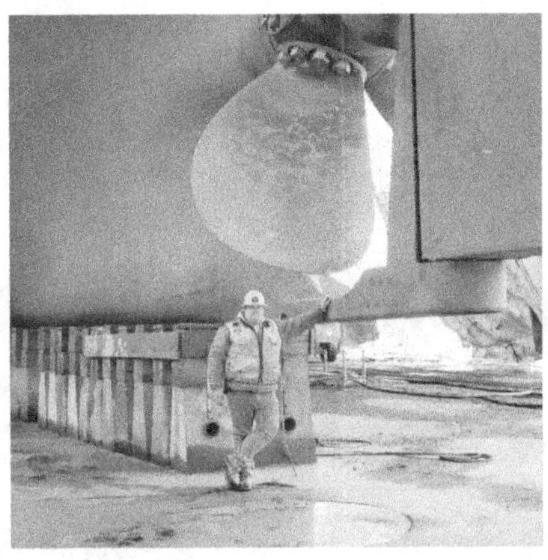

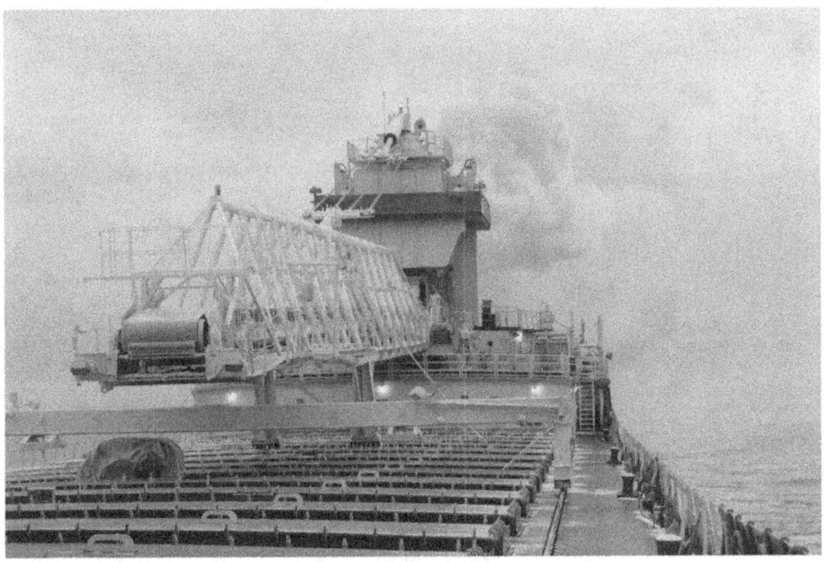

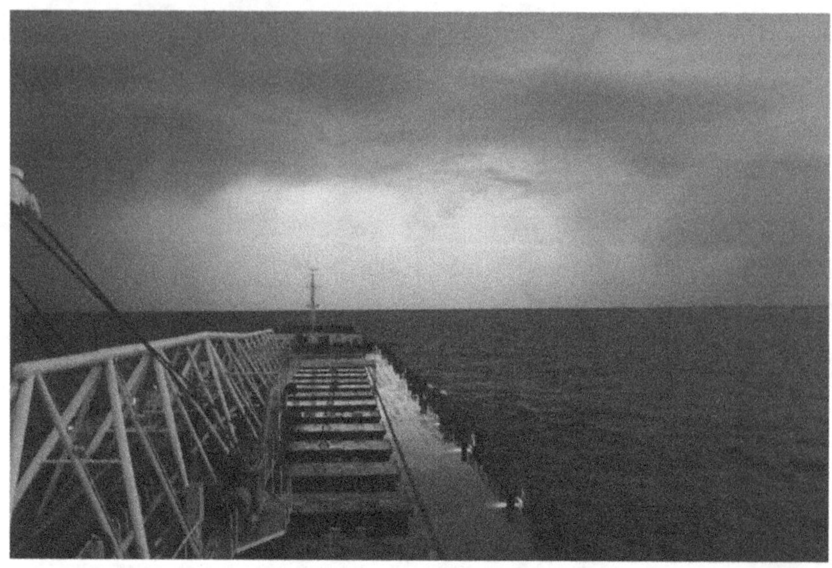

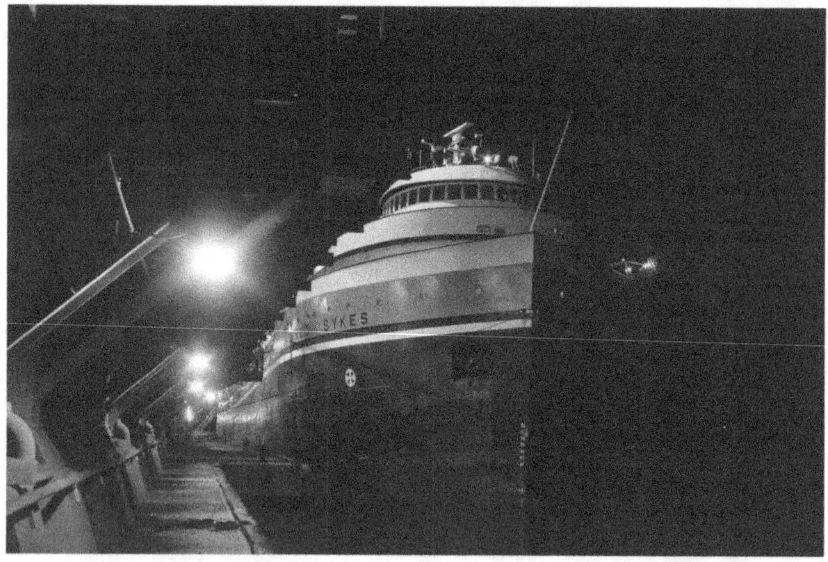

I started noticing that Bob would occasionally post Black & White photos on Facebook. It takes an artistic eye to catch images in B&W that look good, but Bob seems to have that talent. Here are some that he offered:

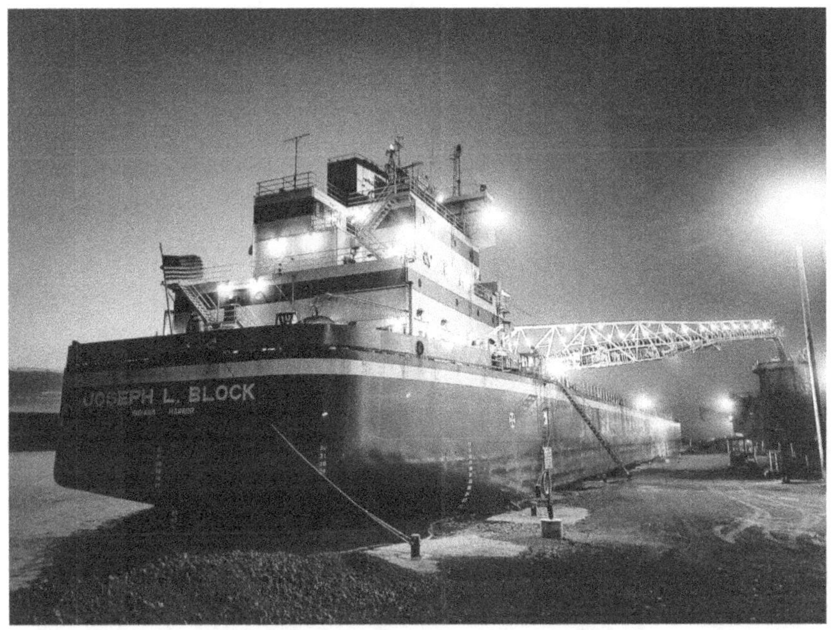

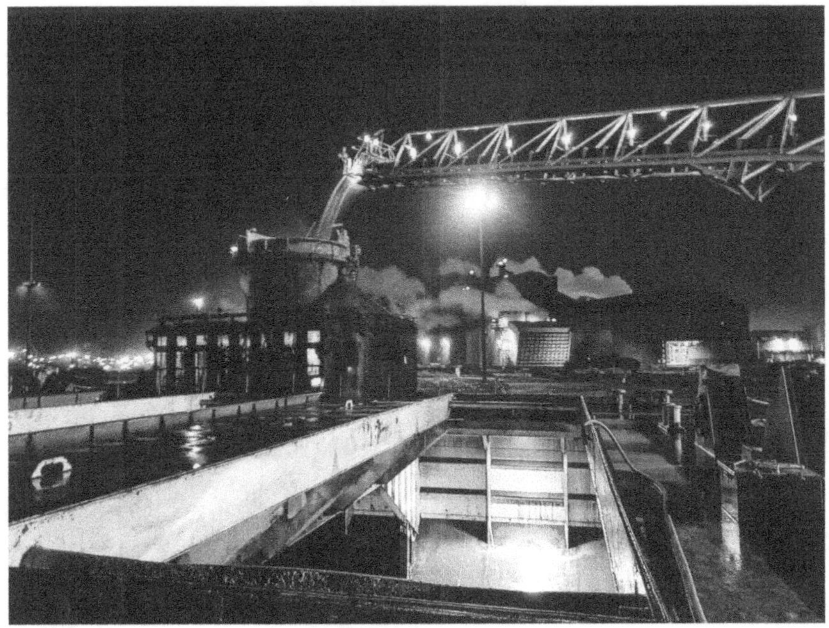

Another one of Bob's interests is steam locomotives. I think Bob Haworth will eventually put together his own books of photographs in both Great Lakes ships, as well as the history of steam locomotives.

19

Shipboard Wedding

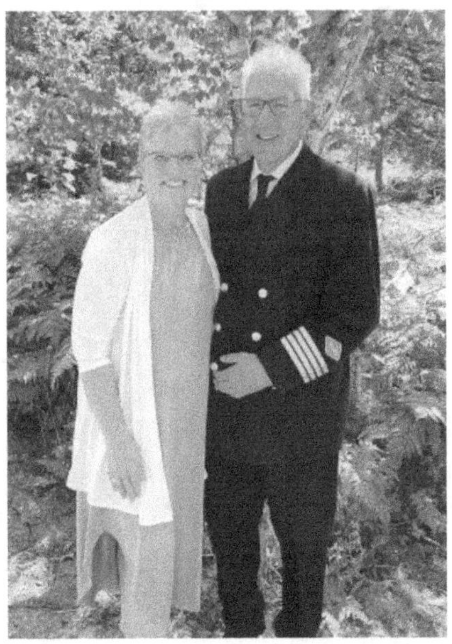

Bob Haworth was sailing on the "Joe Block" when Peggy & Ray were married. He was one of the photographers at the wedding, but I don't know if any of Bob's pictures are included here.

<u>Peggy Captain</u>

One of the more unusual sailor and wife couples on the Great Lakes is Peggy O'Connell and her husband, Captain Ray Sheldon. Many Great Lakes Boat Nerds who follow Facebook will recognize Peggy's posts as **PEGGY CAPTAIN.**

Peggy and Ray met in 2009 when Ray dropped off a flag to be repaired at her sign shop in Escanaba. When Ray came in to pick up the flag, she asked for a tour of the *Joseph L. Block* (and didn't charge him for the repair). He granted the tour about a month later and when she was on the tour, she found out that he would occasionally take guests aboard. So, she requested a trip, but it would be 9 years before that would happen.

Peggy was elected to the Escanaba City Council just after the CN Ore dock in Escanaba closed down. Ray, thinking she may be able to help get it re-opened, called and told her it was time to take the trip. In September of 2018, Peggy and Lynn Williams, a mutual friend of theirs, took a ride aboard the *Joe Block*. Peggy and Ray were only acquaintances and it wasn't until February of 2019, shortly after both of their spouses had passed away after many years of health problems, that they started to meet for coffee. After just a few months, on May 5th, with Ray working on the ship most of the time, he called her to the dock at Port Inland and got down on one knee and asked Peggy to marry him. They kissed for the first time that day! Then they met with their pastor and decided on a December wedding.

A few weeks later on June 5th, Ray called Peggy and said, "Why are we waiting? Come over to the boat when I come into Port Inland at the end of the month, and we will get married!" She said, "Okay!"

So, On June 30th, 2019, Captain Raymond Sheldon became the first working Great Lakes Captain to get married aboard his working ship. They didn't know about this until later, when they did some research. A retired captain, Gerald Coughlin and his wife Joan, married on the Paul R. Tregurtha in 1992, and I'm sure there are others, sailors and guests, but thus far it appears that Ray and Peggy made history.

The wedding became even more unusual when another ship got into Port Inland just ahead of Ray's, and he had to anchor a mile off the dock. The only way to get the wedding party to the ship, including Pastor Aaron Anderson and his wife Roxanna, the matron of honor Renee Kadish and her husband Aaron, and photographer Michael Hall, was by launching the fast rescue boat.

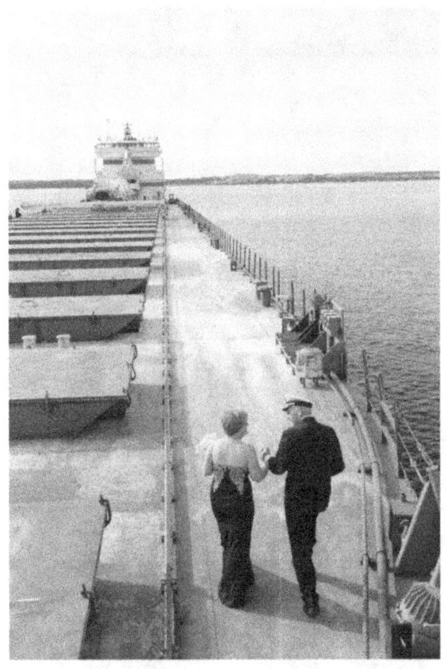

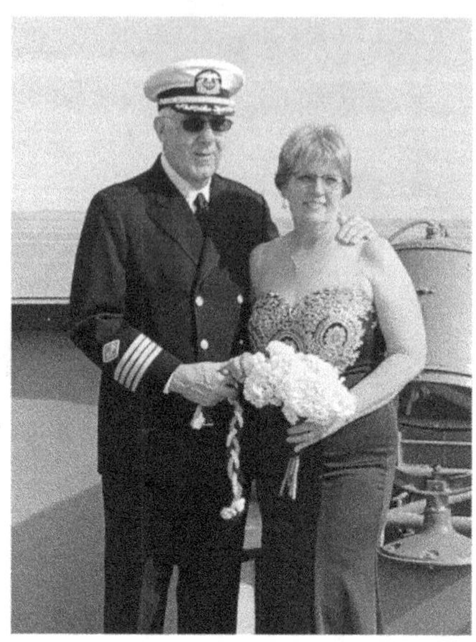

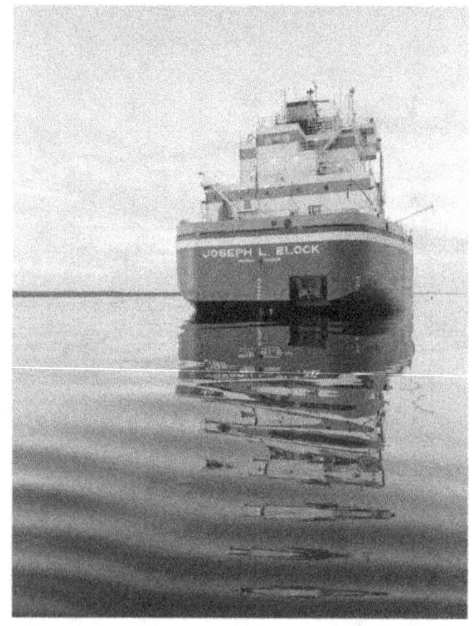

M/V "Joseph L. Block"

It took three trips to accomplish this. First Mate John T. Olson served as the best man and other crew members participated as well. Will English was the "ring bearer" and Bob Haworth recorded the ceremony live on Facebook.

At the end of a beautiful day, the ship went into the dock and everyone except the bride went ashore. This would be the first of many trips she would take that year. During 2020, Peggy followed the ship around the lakes and they visited all the lighthouses, beaches, and waterfalls they could find. Ray even saw the Rock Cut in the St. Mary's River for the first time by land.

Ray retired in March of 2021 after 44.5 years with the same fleet. It was a career that began with Inland Steel and ended with Cleveland Cliffs, even though he never left the fleet.

The couple continues to find new adventures in travel and work. Peggy obtained her merchant mariner's credential in November of 2021 so that they could work together, and take advantage of opportunities to work and travel aboard ships.

In the winter of 2022, Ray worked for Sarter Marine Towing in Sturgeon Bay, Wisconsin, bringing in ships for layup and dry-docking. Peggy was on the tugs as well with her camera.

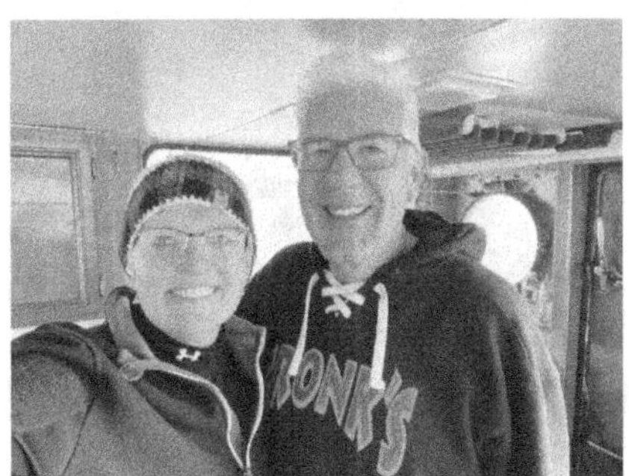

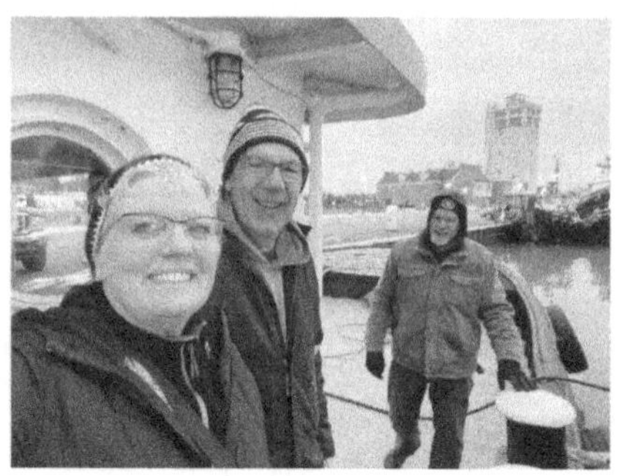

In the summer of 2022, they began working as Captain (Ray) and Narrator (Peggy)with *The Original Soo Locks Boat Tours* in Sault Ste. Marie, MI. They love working with Interlake Steamship who just purchased the tour boats after 88 years of being operated by the Welch family.

Peggy sold her businesses but still has one account that brings them home every few weeks. She makes decals for Jorde Decals in Rochester, MN, for tractor restoration. Ray works alongside her in this business.

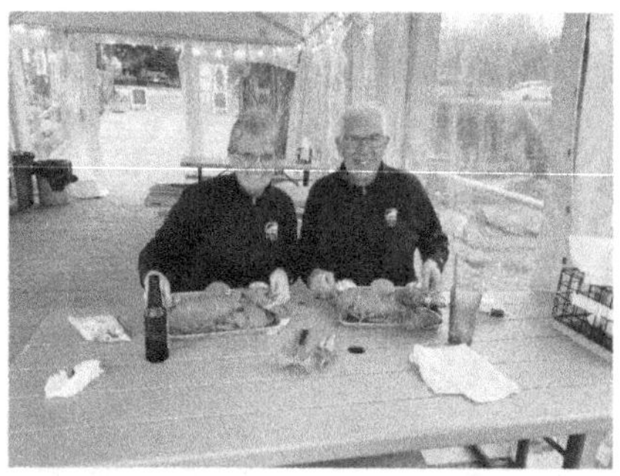

You can follow their adventures on Peggy's Facebook page **Peggy Captain, Mr. and Mrs. Captain's Adventures,** or on Instagram, *mrscaptain5461*. Peggy posts many videos and photos that are from a unique perspective of being aboard.

20

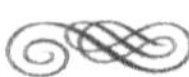

UNUSUAL SAILORS

There are some Great Lakes sailors who don't quite fit the mold of the picture I painted in the original Sweetwater Sailors , the lifelong mariners, dedicated to their careers as a sailor. Some of those are presented in this chapter.

Father Jack Harper

One of my high school classmates, Dave Harper, asked me to send him two autographed copies of my book, Sweetwater Sailors. He asked that I personalize the second book for his brother, Jack. Jack was several years younger than me and Dave, and I may have met him when I hunted with the Harper family one time during high school, but I didn't remember him. According to Dave, Jack became a Diocesan priest in northern Wisconsin.

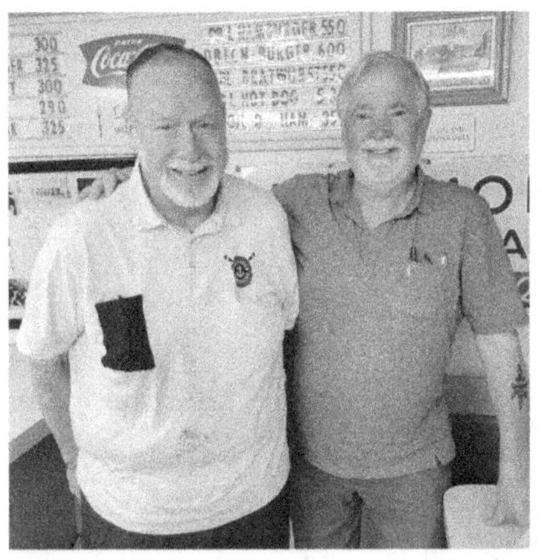

I asked Dave why his brother would want a copy of the book, and Dave told me that Jack had sailed on the Great Lakes before he went to the Seminary. I figured Jack may have sailed for a summer, or maybe one season, but I contacted Father Jack and found out that he had sailed for six seasons with Interlake Shipping. Father Jack is now retired and still living in northern Wisconsin, so I met up with him at Micky Lu's in Marinette, as shown in the picture here.

I asked Jack to send me some of his memories from his time sailing, and story that follows is what he shared. He wrote the titles himself, and it appears Father Jack is a great creative writer. I like Jack's thoughtful perspective, much of which I also experienced when I was young and naïve, because of my sheltered, northern Wisconsin childhood.

An Emptiness Never to be Fed

The calm silence was to some degree tangible; mumbled morning greetings barely audible. It was November 11, 1975, and we were in Muskegon Harbor, having sought shelter from the vicious foreboding sea. The S.S. *Edmund Fitzgerald* had fallen victim to the torturous wind and waves with the loss of 29 of our shipmates! Life is light and relaxed most of our days and then, with very little warning, the waters which seduce us rise, roll, and drown us. The risk remains ever present; the beauty continues to draw us and we remember, but continue to take large amounts of money for much more than we have done!

It's a Trap...

And before we understand, it's too late. We've heard that the Great Lakes sailors make big money. Very similarly, the Philippine candidates for cruise ship employment seek an opportunity to find a better financial life. They attend a cruise ship introduction workshop, learn English, and wait for a call. The call comes and they fly away from a lifestyle they will never again experience! They make 5 to 10 times the wages they've ever made. Soon they are supporting their own family, then their family of origin, with some college tuition thrown in, and then his mother and father-in-law, and his wife's brothers and sisters. The Great Lakes sailors buy a winter home in Florida, a new car (mine was a Corvette), and a richer social status, with the clothes, dining, and drinking to match. The trap rarely experiences an escape....

Talk About Encounter!

In the mid-70s, I was sailing as a Second Cook on an Interlake ship (the name escapes me). Then there was a crew change, and my new roommate was a 50-year-old black man named Willie. Not only had I never known a black man, but the only black men I knew by name were Green Bay Packers! It was a strange collision of cultures, with genuine commitment from both individuals, to make the job the priority. That seemed to be the key, and it worked.

21

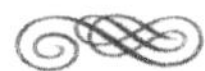

JIM LEGAULT

One of my contacts for my book on Commercial Fishermen put me in contact with Jim Legault, who is well known in Commercial Fishing circles for his great action shots of the boats, the men, and real-life fishing photos. I recognized the Legault name, and found out that Jim was the grandson of my neighbor growing up over in Marinette, Wisconsin. We had never met until these photos were exchanged.

During my conversations with Jim, I found out that he had also sailed on Great Lakes ore carriers for about five years, back in the 1970s. Jim gave me the following story about his memory of being stranded in the ice, as well as some wonderful pictures, and he has graciously given me permission to use the following photographs from his collection.

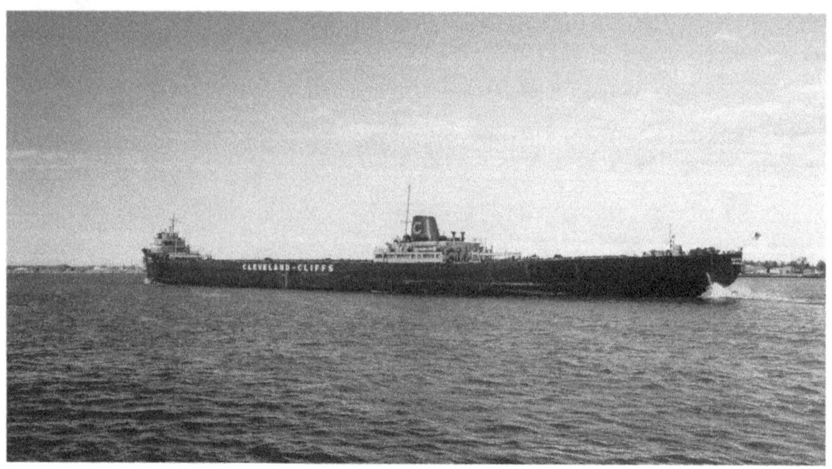

S.S. "Cliffs Victory" - converted WW II Victory ship.

But first, here is Jim's story:

The first blast of winter and an old photo unlocked a few frozen memories of Ore Boat sailing in the first extended sailing season on the Great Lakes in 1977-78. In an attempt to lengthen the sailing season, the Federal Government had agreed to pay the shipping companies for the damages incurred in the experiment. The shipping companies saw it as a potential windfall to fix some of their tired old equipment

I had just finished the work on a book project, was dead broke and needed some quick cash to catch up. A windfall for me too.

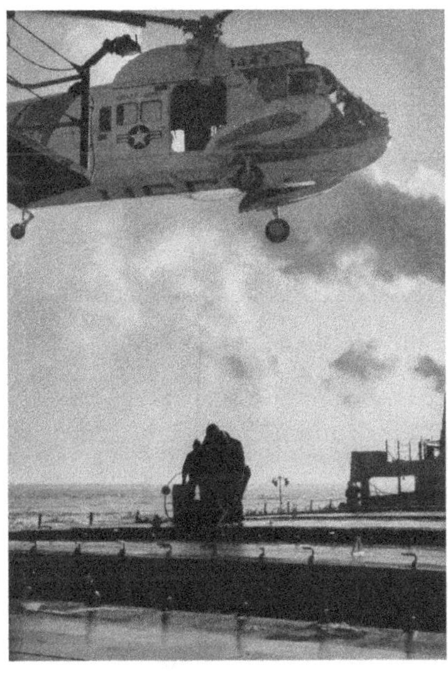

I met the SS Crispin Ogle-bay in Escanaba about the 12th of January, 1978, and after a very slow trip through the Straits of Mackinaw with ice breaker assist (The Mackinaw), we passed through Lake Huron fairly unobstructed.

After another slow trip in the rivers and Lake St Clair, we joined a convoy (6 ships) with the Ice breaker "Northwind" leading us in the western end of Lake Erie. Very slow, but we kept going.

As the convoy approached Cleveland with the last load of the year, we were stopped dead by the ice. It took almost 9 days to make as many miles with Cleveland in sight the whole time. First, all the alcohol was consumed, next all the ice cream, and finally, all the sugar as the alcoholics tried to replace alcohol with sugar.

We anchored behind new ice as wind-rowed ice passed and scrapped by on the port side, driven by easterly strong winds. On the starboard side, solid ice, strong winds, no motion, and the lights of Cleveland. On about day six, a Coast Guard helicopter landed amidship and delivered milk, prime rib, and no alcohol, but more ice cream and cigarettes. The drunks talked about heading out across the ice on foot and it wasn't the whiskey talking.

The reason we were trapped, as I later found out, was that the ice was compressed against the Lake Erie shore by the strong winds. It was due to "a storm of the century" that then caused the wind to shift, and the ice pressure was finally relieved. We tied up on the Cleveland lakefront, the drunks took taxis to the Flats (area of bars and clubs close by), and then the wind blew almost 100-mph and the barometric pressure fell to 28.28 inches (the lowest non tropical atmospheric pressure ever recorded up to that time in the inland US).

The Wiki article below is about the blizzard in the central United States. For the storm which affected the northeastern United States that year, see Northeastern United States Blizzard of 1978.

<u>Morning of January 26, 1978:</u>

The Great Blizzard of 1978, also known as the Cleveland Superbomb,[1] was a historic winter storm that struck the Ohio Valley and Great Lakes from Wednesday, January 25 through Friday, January 27, 1978. The 28.28 inches (958 millibars) barometric pressure measurement recorded in Cleveland, Ohio was the lowest non-tropical atmospheric pressure ever recorded in the mainland United States, up until the Upper Midwest Storm of October 26, 2010 (28.20" measured at 5:13PM CDT at Bigfork Municipal Airport, Bigfork, MN). The lowest central pressure for the 1978 blizzard was 28.05" (953 mb) measured in southern Ontario a few hours after the aforementioned record in Cleveland.[2] On rare occasions, extra-tropical cyclones with central pressures below 28 inches of mercury or about 95 kPa (950 mb) have been recorded in Wiscasset, Maine (27.9") and Newfoundland (27.76").[3]

Here are some of Jim Legault's photos, taken during his sailing years:

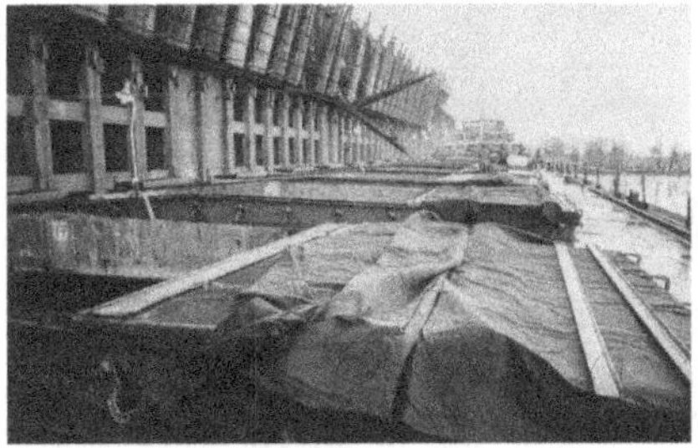

Loading iron ore

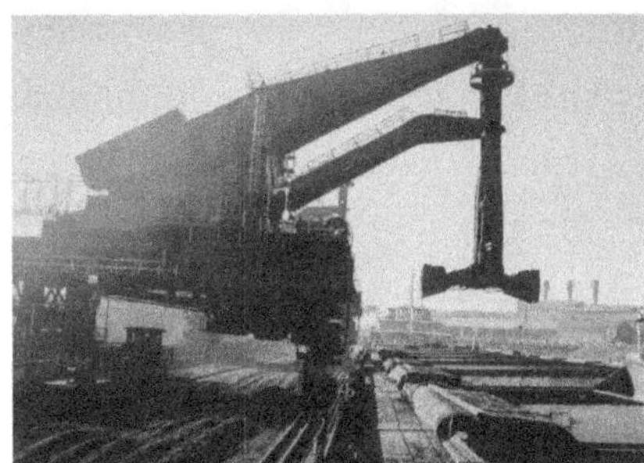

Unloading at a steel mill, using the Hulett Unloader System buckets. The operator sat in that small white area just above the bucket. They tended to be more careful than operators using clamshell buckets, hanging from cables, because if the Hulett hit the ship's hatch coaming, it shook the operator when it made contact.

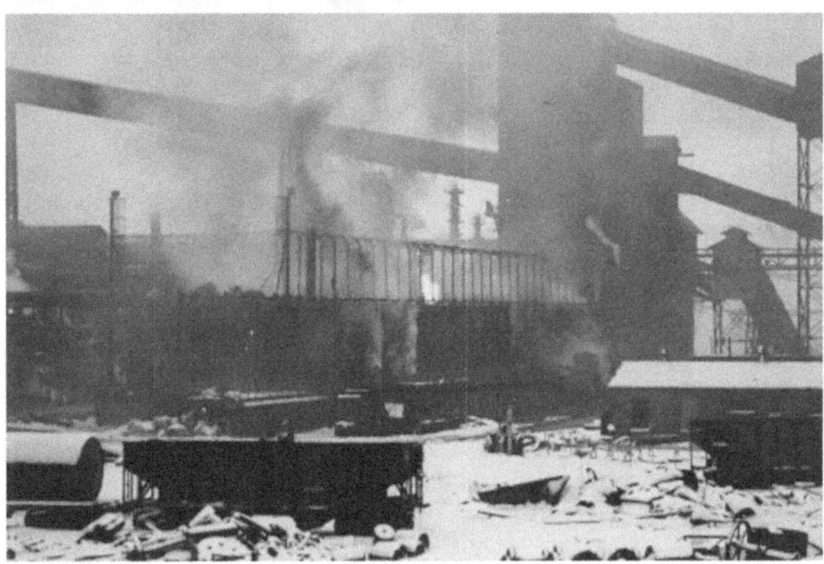

Good B&W picture of a large steel mill in operation. The sailors were breathing in all those vapors.

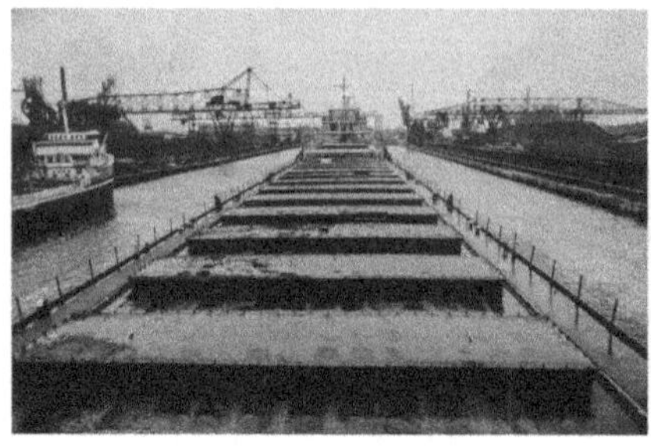

Pictures of these tight rivers and harbors always amaze me. The talent of the average Great Lakes captains to navigate these narrow waterways, with minimal damage, is truly amazing.

Jim Legault also spent a lot of time at Bay Shipbuilding Company in Sturgeon Bay, taking photographs for a Safety project they were working on. The following photos are from that project, during the building of the Edwin H. Gott.:

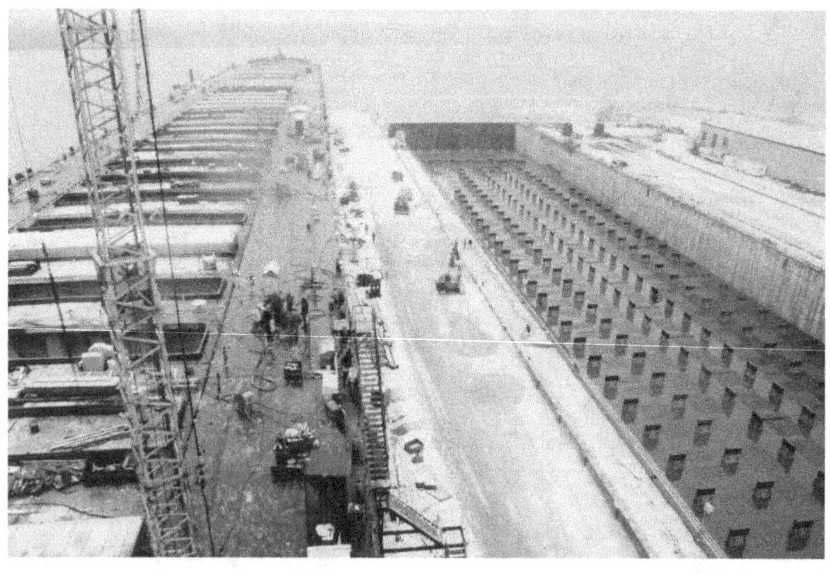

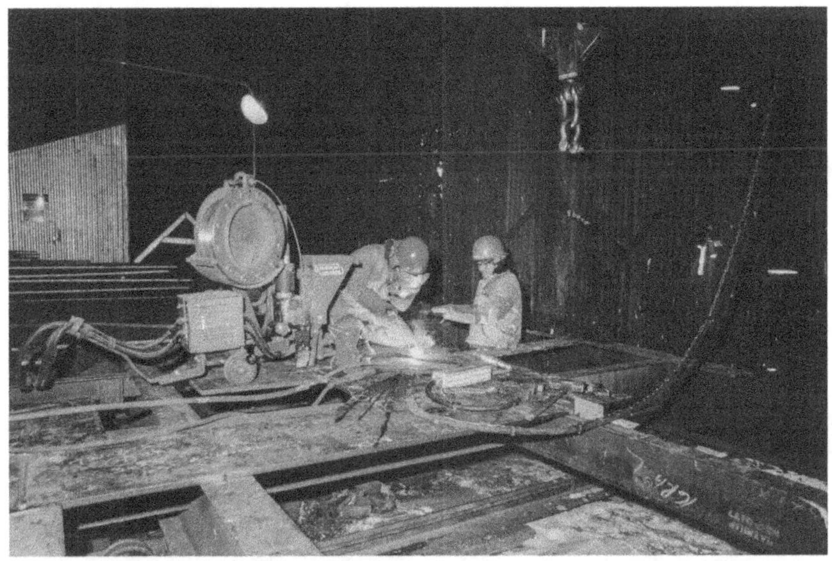

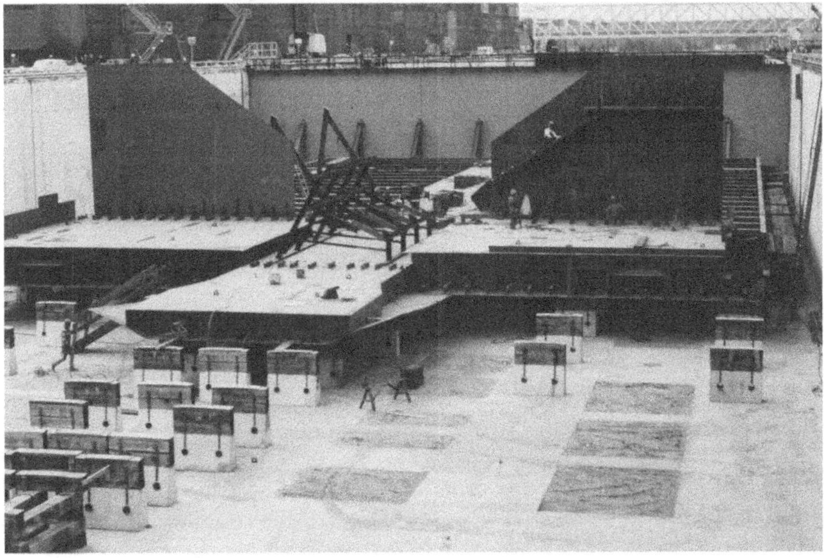

22

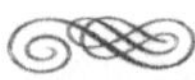

JON HELD

<u>From the Great Lakes to the Arctic and Antarctic</u>

The following stories are from a man who only sailed the Great Lakes for a short time, as a teenager. Jonathan (Jon) Held only sailed for one summer, but says that experience affected the course of his life.

Jon is married to a friend of Ann's (my wife), whom I recently met. It was through Jon's wife that I found out that Jon had bought a copy of my first book, Sweetwater Sailors, in addition to one of my Autobiographical Books, with stories about my world travels as a Marine Surveyor. I also heard that Jon was a Coast Guard veteran, so obviously, I wanted to meet him and learn more about his experiences.

I was not aware of Jon's Great Lakes sailing experience at the time, but soon learned that his uncle had sailed for Reiss Coal as a Chief Engineer, so when Jon was looking for a summer job, he went to the Union Hall in Duluth and ended up getting a job with Reiss.

Jon told me he was surprised that he was given details of how this position became available. Apparently, the man he was replacing had been decapitated by an accidental cable whiplash. Jon joined that ship and was immediately thrown into shipboard duties, riding the Bos'n chair, along with other tasks, without any real training or safety instructions. That was the way things were back in "the old days," before the maritime unions took an active role.

The following are Jon's memories of his varied career. He didn't stay on the Great Lakes as a Merchant Mariner, but traces his first maritime experiences to the Great Lakes.

Childhood Memories

Growing up in Sheboygan, Wisconsin, as a preschooler, I spent time with my dad many days because he worked the second shift. He would take me with him in the morning and we would go to the river to talk to the commercial fishermen. The fishermen went out early in the morning to pull their gill nets and came in loaded with their catch of perch. After lunch, they went out again and came back in the afternoon with a second load. That was in the "glory years," when the fish were plentiful.

On other days, we might find coal boats in the harbor or a clay boat bringing clay for the Kohler company, which they then used to make toilets and sinks. The clay boats came from the Cliffs of Dover across the Atlantic. There was great excitement in Sheboygan when a boat came in. When the ship's whistle blew, people came from all over town to watch them come into the harbor. Watching the coal being unloaded with the big overhead crane was also exciting for a young boy. It might take almost a day for the boat to unload. Later, the self-unloading boats came with their conveyor booms, which finished much faster. When the boats left, they needed to turn around. This often required a tugboat to assist them, which added more excitement to the event.

On other days, we went to the Coast Guard station for a visit. Everyone was very friendly and showed us the boats and equipment and explained how everything worked. There was usually something good to eat as well.

I was fascinated by the small boats at the Coast Guard station in Sheboygan. They had a 36-foot motor lifeboat back then, which had a heavy brass weight at the bottom to right it, if it rolled over in the surf. They normally had a crew of four and space for 12 survivors in a forward cabin.

In earlier years, there was a lookout tower on a pier, out off of the station. This was manned 24 hours a day, 365 days a year. They scanned the lake for vessels or persons in distress, which might occur during stormy conditions. The motto was: 'You have to go out, but you don't have to come back.' Time spent at that Coast Guard station had a large effect on my eventual enlistment in the Coast Guard in 1968."

My Summer on the Great Lakes

In 1964, at the age of 19, I was trying to figure out what I wanted to do with my life. I had tried factory work and the local university center, but neither one of those jobs excited me. Then I met a new friend whose dad oversaw the hiring process at the C. Reiss Coal Company in Sheboygan. He also hired people for their steamships. The steamships hauled coal and grain all over the Great Lakes.

I applied and later got a letter of commitment stating that Reiss steamship would hire me. All I needed to do next was go to the Milwaukee Coast Guard office to get my Merchant Mariner's license. Once that arrived, I had to sign up at a union hall, which meant a trip to Chicago or Duluth. I chose Duluth because I had never been there before.

In March, I took the trip to Duluth, in my 1956 VW Beetle, with a good friend. We did not have a lot of money, so we spent the night at a state park, sleeping on picnic tables to be off the ground. We awoke to several inches of snow in the morning. Mind you, there was not much heat in the 1956 VW in March!

After about a month, I got a call from the union hall. A ship in Chicago was coming to Sheboygan with iron ingots for the Kohler Company, and they needed a deckhand. The ship was the "Otto M. Reiss," built in 1906. She was steam-powered and not exactly the queen of the fleet. The deckhand I was to replace had died aboard ship when he was decapitated by a steel cable. This unusual start at a job was even more strange when I signed on to the ship at midnight on Friday the 13th. Good thing I'm not superstitious!

My time on the "Otto Reiss" was interesting and definitely an adventure, and the work was hard at times. Soon after getting aboard, we passed through the Soo Locks, which was the first of many such trips. As the new deckhand, it was part of my job to be lowered over the side on a Bos'n chair. This was just a piece of 2 x 4 wood, tied to a rope that went through a boom to swing the man out over the side of the ship to the dock. I was lowered from the moving boat to the dock, and the trick was to get off the Bos'n chair before being dragged along the dock. Fortunately, I managed to get off without any mishap.

We usually hauled grain from Duluth to either Cleveland or Buffalo, and then loaded coal in Toledo to take back to Superior, Wisconsin. This was a "milk run," which was repeated over and over. The only big difference from one trip to the next was the weather. Most of the storms seemed to be on Lake Superior, and although I never experienced a November storm on Superior, I can imagine what it would be like.

As a deckhand, I had many duties. I was a day worker, mostly, which meant an 8-hour workday and then 16 hours off. Most of the crew worked 4 hours on and 8 hours off. My work included cleaning the cargo hold between loads, keeping the forward berthing area and living spaces clean, and whatever else needed doing. The cargo hold cleaning was done with shovels, brooms, and a firehose. The hose had a lot of pressure and could push you around if you lost control of it.

When the hold was full, we had to close the hatch covers. These were large steel telescoping covers that were pulled shut with a steam-powered winch and required a steel cable stretched across the deck. The space on deck between the hatch openings was about 3-feet, with many tripping hazards. If anyone tripped and fell into an empty hold, they would not survive the 40-foot fall onto a steel deck. So, great care was required, especially when underway in rough weather.

On the positive side, the crew was friendly and were a great help to the new guys. And the food! I could have steak for breakfast if I wanted. We had choices at every meal and always had fresh pies and cakes. The bad part was that I lived forward, and the galley and mess deck were located in the after part of the ship. In bad weather, we had to walk while wearing a harness attached to a long wire, from the forward end to the after end, to prevent us from being swept over the side by large waves.

Oceanography School

In 1966, I went to the Southern Maine Vocational Technical Institute in South Portland, Maine, to study oceanography, marine biology, ship deck operations, and engine room procedures. Our school ship was a wooden World War II minesweeper. We had several cruises where we practiced oceanographic data collection as well as ship operations. I learned a lot about life on the Atlantic.

I had always wanted to see Maine, and now I had two years to see the sights. Most weekends, I toured the coast and sometimes ventured inland. Training centered on Marine Sciences and Shipboard Operations. The first semester, we had both deck and engine room classes. Then we chose one to concentrate on, and I chose the engine room. On our various cruises, we stood watches and, with supervision, actually ran the ship. There were also oceanographic operations while underway. What I learned here paid off in a big way when I joined the Coast Guard.

One of my best memories was the building of the replica of the schooner "*America.*" Rudolph Schaefer, owner of Schaefer Brewing in New York, had a replica of the original "*America*" (winner of the first Americas Cup Race in England) built at Gaudy and Stevens shipyard in East Boothbay, Maine. I went there on weekends to see the progress. She is a magnificent vessel, long and sleek, and very fast. On May 3, 1967, she was launched on the Damariscotta River, with hundreds of people cheering.

After graduation in June 1968, I returned to Sheboygan to decide where to use my newfound knowledge."

<u>U.S. Coast Guard</u>

Shortly after graduation from the school in Maine in 1968, I received a letter from Uncle Sam inviting me to join his Army. I had been in contact with the Coast Guard recruiter in Milwaukee for several months, but he had no openings available, so I took my Army physical and passed with flying colors.

One day in October, I got a call saying that the recruiter had an opening for boot camp in Cape May, New Jersey. I said yes, and four days later, I boarded a plane at O'Hare in Chicago, followed by a bus ride from Philadelphia to Cape May. A bunch of us collected at a restaurant for burgers and after a while, a fellow came in to say that he was from the training center and asked us if we were ready. He seemed very friendly and polite. We boarded the bus, and once the door closed, the whole world changed!

While in Boot Camp, I learned that the rank of Aerographer's Mate (weatherman) had been changed to Marine Science

Technician, which combined weather and oceanography. With my past training, this was a natural choice for me.

After basic training, I was assigned to the 5th Coast Guard District in Baltimore, Maryland, and I reported to the Coast Guard Cutter "*Westwind*," a polar icebreaker. The ship was half taken apart for repairs between trips at the time I boarded. A normal north-trip to Thule, Greenland, was from about May to September. A trip south to the Antarctic was about November to May. Between trips, it was rebuild time. We did this because icebreakers get a lot of wear and tear. I made trips to Thule in 1969 and twice in 1970, once in May and the other in November. Twenty-four hours of darkness and -70°F air temperature! From there, we went to the Antarctic via the Panama Canal.

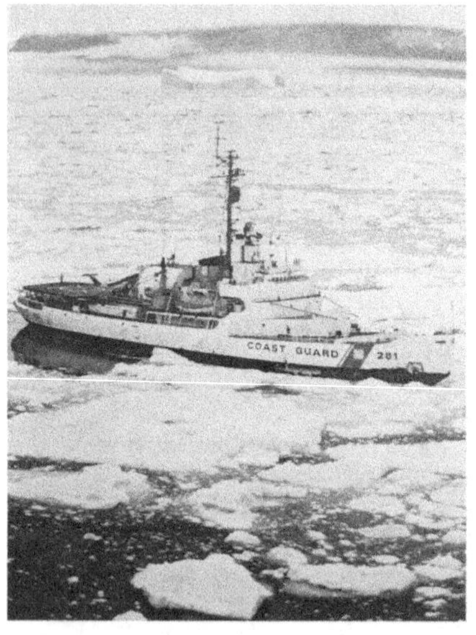

Being aboard an icebreaker, where a lot of oceanographic work occurred, I advanced rapidly. The work was very interesting, and we had many people from the university doing research aboard. One year, we had a film crew from National Geographic aboard, doing an article on the Coast Guard. That is where the pictures of me setting up explosive charges to free the ship from the ice came from.

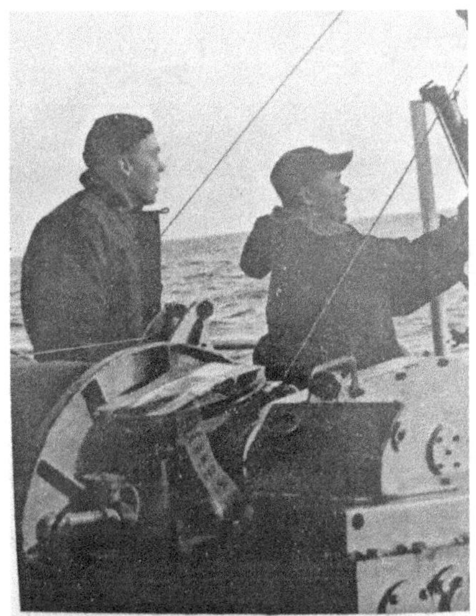

Jon is on the left in both of these photos, performing his Oceanographic duties aboard the CGC 'Westwind'.

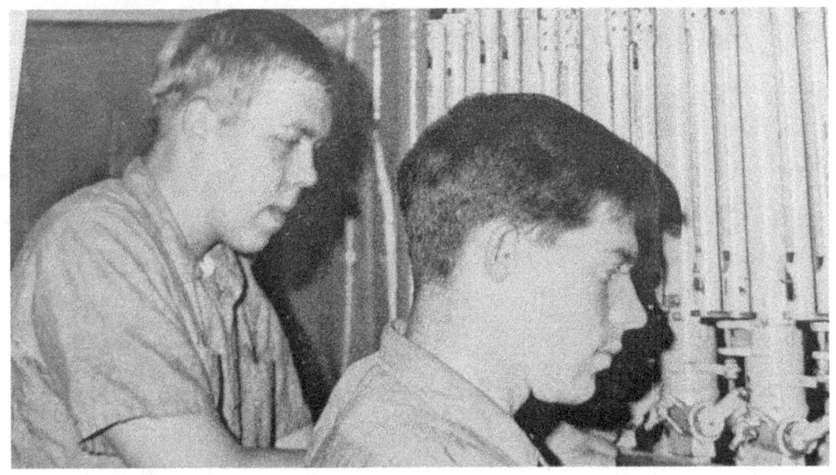

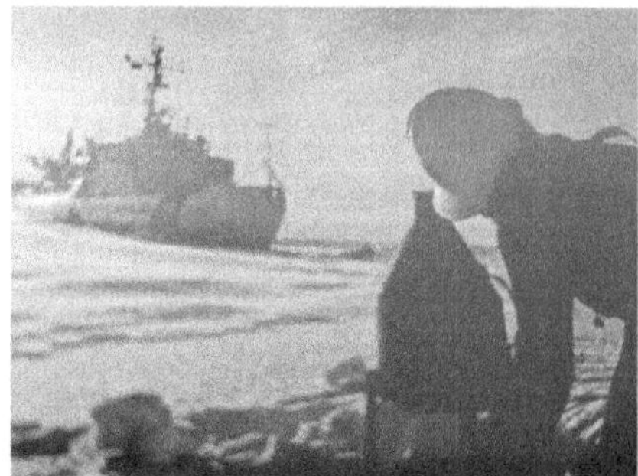

In this photo, Jon Held is setting explosive charges to open a "lane" in the ice for the CGC 'Westwind' to proceed through thick ice.

I was a scuba diver aboard the *Westwind*. We did routine hull inspections, and also inspected the 17-foot diameter, stainless steel propellers for damage. There were dives to count sea life, and other Marine Biology type projects. Also, divers were used to recover articles that rolled off deck or fell off other ships. Diving in 27° seawater in a wetsuit was a "chilling" experience, but it gave me an extra $90 per month. That was huge, since I only made about $75 a month regular pay.

Some unique experiences in the Coast Guard were the crossing ceremonies. The first one was the Arctic Circle, and those of us crossing for the first time had to become polar bears. This required a lot of strange activities, including a haircut by the Royal Barber, crawling through a tunnel with nondescript items in it and ultimately facing King Neptune, and kissing the Baby's Belly. We also had our noses painted blue. It was all in fun, and a needed break from the daily routine of a 7-month trip. On our trip south, we crossed the equator and the Antarctic Circle, which had similar antics. That also included a trip through the Panama Canal.

Our trip through the Panama Canal was unbelievable. The plant life seemed lush, and the leaves were huge. Upon entry to the first set of locks from the Atlantic, we met a Russian freighter coming out. This was Christmas Eve in 1969, and things were rather tense when the 'Stars and Stripes' faced the 'Hammer and Sickle.' At that time, Russian ship crewmen had their families aboard. Laundry hung from lines on deck. A little blond girl aboard their ship was staring at us and suddenly yelled out, 'Merry Christmas.' This broke the tension, and people on both ships began to wish each other Merry Christmas. It was a great moment between two countries with different beliefs. The passage through the Canal was fascinating.

From the Coast Guard Cutter "*Westwind*," I went to Governors Island, New York, to be an instructor at the Marine Science Technician school. This was a great duty. I lived on base, just off the southern tip of Manhattan, between the Brooklyn Bridge and the Statue of Liberty. It was like getting an 18-month paid vacation in New York City. Because of the Vietnam War, there was a lot of dislike for U.S. military at that time. One afternoon, everyone on the base had to report to the movie theater. A bomb threat had been called in and the theater had been searched. But we watched "Alice's Restaurant" three times while the rest of the base was searched. Nothing was found.

Being in New York meant lots of time ashore. So many things to see and do. That also included Mystic Seaport in Connecticut and several weekend trips to Boston, New Hampshire, and Vermont."

Wood Boatbuilding School

After my discharge from the Coast Guard, I decided to go to a wooden boatbuilding school in Lubec, Maine. This was on the coast, almost into Canada. Because I had very much enjoyed my time in

Maine during my previous oceanography school experience, this was an obvious choice for me.

I found the Wooden Boatbuilding program at Washington County Vocational Technical Institute in Lubec.Classes were held in an old Coast Guard lifeboat station, so I was right at home. Near the water was a boathouse with a marine railway to launch and haul boats. I learned a lot about lofting (drawing the boat full size on the floor), cutting out the many parts, and then assembling them into a boat. I also met several people that I stayed in touch with for many years.

We learned the basics and began building boats right away. We had two instructors; one was a British naval architect who was all about math and detailed drawings, and the other was a local lobsterman, whose family had built boats for many generations. His method was to carve a boat from a block of cedar until '*it looked right*.' He would then take measurements from the model and scale it up to full size. Both instructors were very good, but they just had different methods. We were lucky to have both. I really enjoyed the people in Maine and the simple lifestyle.

After the school in Maine, I returned to Sheboygan and eventually settled into a career as an electrician. I started working at the hospitals in town and in 1985 I took a job with the city of Sheboygan. We took care of traffic signals, streetlights, city parks, and all the city's buildings. I did this for 25 years.

After Retirement

After I retired, I enjoyed building wooden boats. Our home in Sheboygan had a three-car garage. One stall was for my wife's car, one for mine, and one for boat building. I spent many happy hours building a half-dozen boats over several years.

Eventually, my wife and I moved to Lake Geneva, Wisconsin, to be near children and grandchildren. Lake Geneva has many pleasure craft on the lake, and Gage Marine is one of the largest companies on Lake Geneva, both operating excursion vessels, selling pleasure craft, and repairing vessels of all kinds. I applied for a job at Gage Marine and have had the opportunity to work with them on wooden boat repairs and the refurbishing of wooden boats.

My spare time is now devoted to building scale model boats, some of which are radio controlled, and they are used on a nearby pond. Some people spend their spare time looking at cars, aircraft, women, etc. I enjoy looking at boats. Anything from a tiny rowboat to an ocean liner. My preference is wood. After all, '*God entrusted the future of mankind to a wooden boat.*'

23

⁂

MARINE CONSTRUCTION

When I worked with the American Bureau of Shipping (ABS) back in the 1970s & 80s, I surveyed a lot of tugs and barges involved in the Great Lakes Marine Construction business. I was relatively inexperienced with vessel operations and maintenance, so, I was always asking questions. I was lucky to have met some fellas working for some of those companies who were close to my age, and they were willing to give me good answers. I learned a lot from them. Therefore, I wanted to include some of them in this book, because they are an important part of the Great Lakes maritime industry. Some of the stories take place off the Lakes, but you'll see why I wanted them included, after you read them.

Dennis (Denny) Kempen is one of those "unusual" Great Lakes sailors I've known for many years. I first met Denny when I was working as an ABS Surveyor, back in the mid-70s. I believe it may have been when several deck barges (B-barges owned by Bultema Dock & Dredge) broke loose in a storm and washed up on the Lake Michigan shoreline. I was one of the ABS Surveyors handling the Damage Surveys, and Denny was one of my points of contact.

I was relatively new with ABS at that time, and I always looked for an experienced guy who was willing to let me 'pick his brain,' and Denny was the guy I chose to answer all of my questions.

When we think of Great Lakes sailors, most people only think of those on the Lake freighters, carferries, and maybe some of the larger tugs. However, the marine construction companies that build and repair break-waters and other marine structures, are exposed to the same weather, and in much smaller vessels. The construction crews not only work inside the harbors, but they do some long-distance lake towing in order to deliver stone, equipment, and supplies to the work sites.

Denny gave me a lot of great experiences from his nearly forty years of working marine construction. Some of the stories were very technical in nature, which may not be as interesting to the average reader, but because this book is intended to be historical in some aspects, I wanted all of Denny's stories to be included. What I decided to do was place those more technically oriented stories in an Appendix at the back of the book. Included are Denny's memories of how the equipment and procedures have changed over the years in the marine construction business. So, please take a look at those stories, and if you want to skip them, I just didn't want you to miss the following details about Denny Kempen.

Denny is from Michigan, and spent his career working for Michigan-based contractors, but he did travel for some unusual jobs, as you will see below. The following background and various stories/experiences are in Denny's words:

24

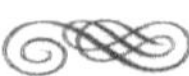

DENNY KEMPEN

My career in marine construction started in 1975 after graduating from Michigan Technological University with a bachelor's degree in civil engineering, in 1974. Jobs were hard to find during that time. Then I received an offer from Bultema Dock and Dredge, based in Muskegon, MI, to be an engineer on a break wall project in Lexington, Michigan. I was told to go to their jobsite and meet Mark Klemp, the Project Engineer, who would tell me what he needed me to do. I loaded my suitcases and headed south from Ontonagon. My plan was to get a motel room for the night and go to the site in the morning, but there was a weekend event in progress, so all the motels were booked. The motel's desk clerk let me stay at her son's treehouse, which had a couch and TV, until Monday when rooms would be available. I accepted.

The next day, I went to the jobsite trailer and met Mark Klemp, Project Engineer, and Don Olsen, Project Superintendent. While filling out my paperwork, they asked me if I knew how to operate an outboard motor. I said I never had, and I could see that 'oh boy' look in their eyes. Mark took me around the site, introducing me and showing me things that might kill me. My jobs were to do some surveying layout, doing cross sections using a sounding basket (I had never heard of, or seen one before).

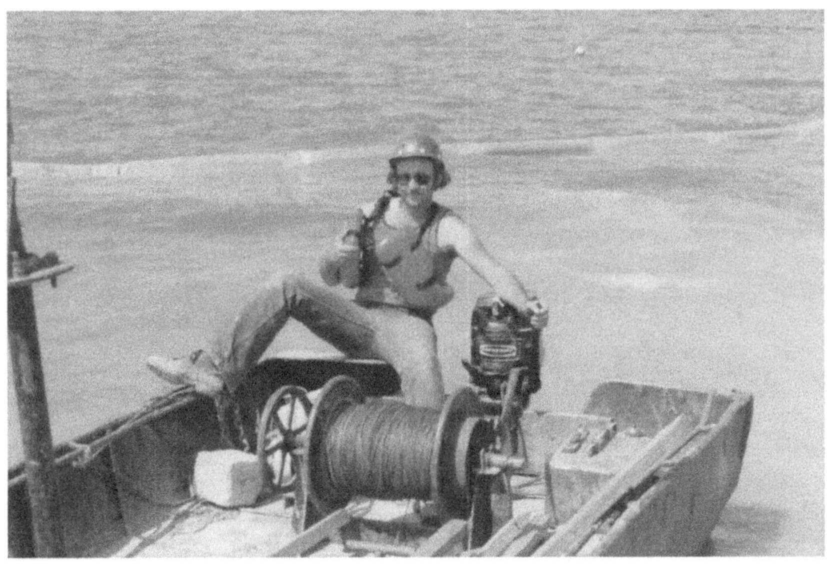

They were using the crane barge 'Wisconsin' with a 1948-built, Model 2400 Lima crane, operated by George Buckner. Mark warned me that George was blind in one eye, so I needed to make sure that he saw me while working around the crane. One day, someone had tied up our steel workboat alongside the barge on George's blind side and when he swung the stone grapple next to the barge, so that the crew could paint depth marks on the crane cables, he lowered the grapple into the workboat, sinking it.

The following picture shows Denny (on the right) with one of their divers, Ron Dahlke. Ron had just come out of the water, taken off his dry suit, and was having a cup of coffee. It was cold, as you could tell from Denny's clothing, but divers can be a bit weird, as well as tough.

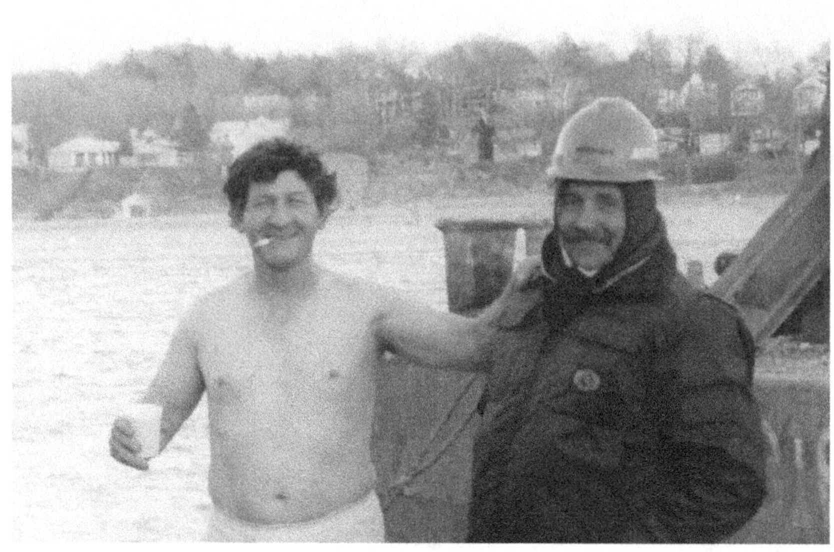

When the lake was too rough to work, they would tow the crane barge north to Port Sanilac for safe harbor. Late one afternoon, when they were making up the tow for the 12-mile tow, Don Olsen asked if I wanted to ride the tug with them. It sounded exciting to me. The tug Charlevoix had a Kalhlenberg engine that could run in forward or reverse without the need of a gearbox.

When it started, it would exhaust the neatest smoke rings as each cylinder would start. One day, someone called the fire department because the exhaust gases caught fire and was burning the paint off the stack. It was a fairly common occurrence and would burn itself out. Captain Alan Lakso told me I could stay in the pilothouse on the settee. After a couple of hours, it was dark, and the seas had built to the point that we were taking them over the bow. I asked Alan how long it would take, and he said we were making about

2 mph, so it should be about 6 hours. I fell asleep, and after a few hours, I again asked Alan how we were doing. He told me, 'Better.' We're holding our own, but earlier, we were losing ground.' We finally arrived at Port Sanilac 12 hours later at daylight.

I had a similar experience in Little Traverse Bay, Michigan, where I had been sent to survey a damaged barge at a construction site. Their tug had picked me up on shore and taken me out to the damaged barge, spudded down out in the bay. After a couple of hours, when I was done with the survey, I asked the crew to take me ashore, so I could head home. I was informed that the weather had worsened, and it was too dangerous to dock where my car was located, so they were going to tow the equipment across the bay, into Harbor Springs.

As many of my readers know, I have a huge problem with motion sickness (wrong profession for that!) and I had my Dramamine in my car, which I couldn't get to. So, I decided to sleep during the trip.

I awoke the next morning, expecting to be in Harbor Springs. When I went up to the pilothouse and asked the captain why we were about seven hours into what should have been a two, maybe a three-hour trip, the captain said he had not been able to make any progress during the night without doing more damage to the barge, so he just held his position for a few hours. We were taking 30-degree rolls (which I saw on the inclinometer in the pilothouse), and I was as sick as I'd ever been. Twelve hours after we had begun, we finally docked in Harbor Springs, and the crew drove me back to my car.

Some of Denny's most amazing stories didn't take place on the Great Lakes. Andrie Marine had the right equipment to do some unusual jobs, so, in the following story, they worked in British Columbia, Canada. As Denny describes it, it is difficult for U.S. companies to perform work in Canada. In one case, I worked in a Canadian shipyard as an ABS Surveyor for over 3-months. I never lied when crossing the border, but I was never asked why I was entering Canada (just the "Where were you born?" question in those days). On one trip after visiting home, the officer at the border noticed my hard hat in the back seat, and I spent the next hour being interrogated. I was actually told to leave within one week. ABS got a nasty letter from Canada Immigration about that.

So, please enjoy some of the ridiculous things that Denny had to endure, while working in Castlegar, B.C., Canada and Jacksonville, Florida:

BRILLIANT DAM

In January 2007, Andrie Inc. of Muskegon, MI, received a contract to rent their Flexifloat jack up barge to Skanska-Chant, for use on their dam expansion project at Castlegar, B.C., Canada. They were adding another turbine to the existing Brilliant Dam by tunneling through the rock on one end of the dam and adding a new turbine on the downstream end of the tunnel. They needed the barge fitted with an excavator to remove the rock plug separating the river from the new tunnel and the downstream turbine.

In January 2007, Andrie Inc. of Muskegon, MI, received a contract to rent their Flexifloat jack up barge to Skanska-Chant, for use on their dam expansion project at Castlegar, B.C., Canada. They were adding another turbine to the existing Brilliant Dam by tunneling through the rock on one end of the dam and adding a new turbine on the downstream end of the tunnel. They needed the barge fitted with an excavator to remove the rock plug separating the river from the new tunnel and the downstream turbine.

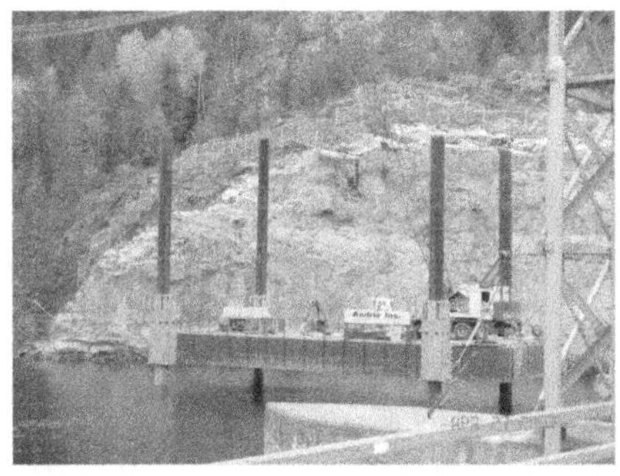

They wanted the Flexifloat barge, which had the capability to jack itself completely out of the water, creating a stable work platform in the swift river currents at the dam. The Flexifloat barge consists of separate 10-foot-wide x 40- or 20-foot-long x 5-foot-deep sections, which are connected together with a simple pin and lock assembly. The 4 spuds are 80 foot long and have a series of flat bars welded on them. The spuds fit in spudwells, fitted with a movable collar and hydraulic cylinders that push against the spud flat bars,   lifting the barge in steps out of the water.

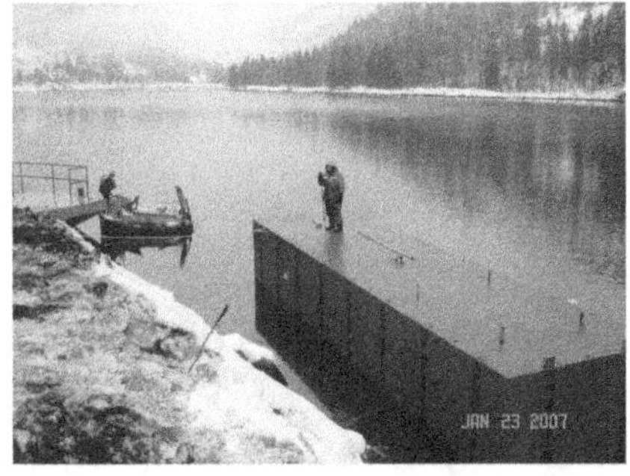

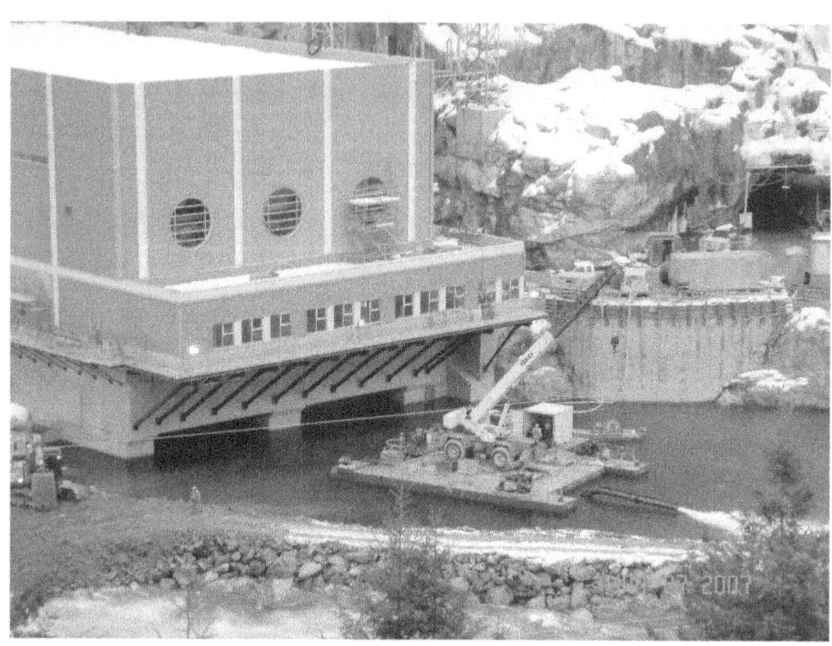

I was chosen to be the first supervisor to go to Castlegar and assemble the barge. My schedule was 30 days in Castlegar and then rotate back home for 30 days. To get permission to work in Canada, I had to fly to Montreal, where they had an immigration office at the airport. There, they processed my paperwork, granting me permission as an advisor who was permitted to oversee work but not able to perform any work that a Canadian citizen could do.

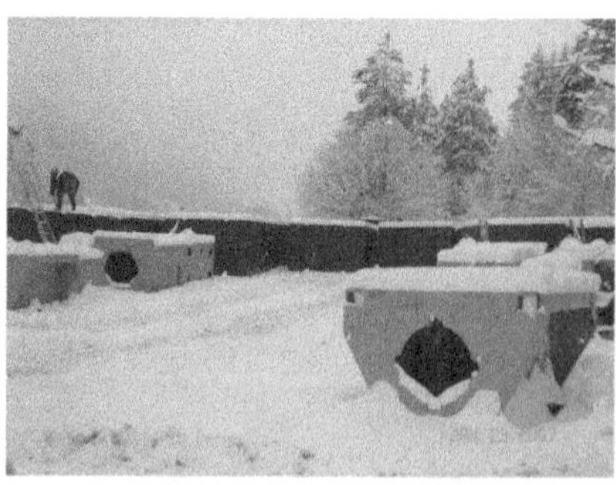

About a week later, the trucks had arrived at the worksite, and I boarded a flight that was to take me to Vancouver, Canada, where I had a connecting flight to Castlegar. When I arrived in Vancouver, my connecting flight had been canceled due to snow at Castlegar. The ticket agent said I could board a flight to a town about 60 miles away, and then rent a car to drive to Castlegar. However, a lady standing behind me in line asked me if I was from Castlegar, and when I told her no, she said if Castlegar was closed for snow, then the alternative of flying to the other town and driving would not work, because the town was on the other side of the mountain and they would close the road for snow, so I would be stranded. I thanked her and booked a flight for the next day.

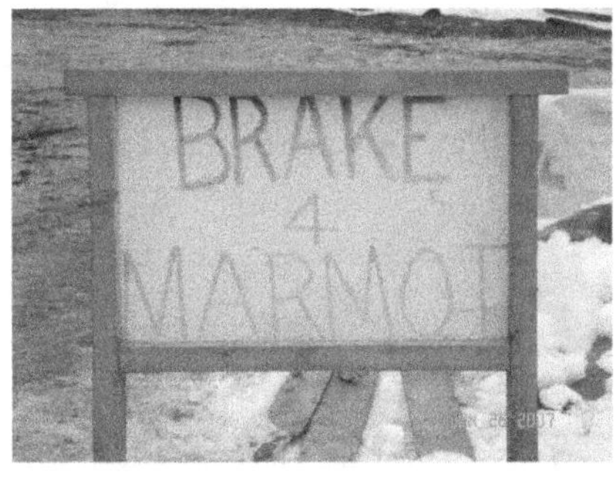

The next day, I arrived at Castlegar and drove to the job-site to check in. On the road to site, I saw a sign that said 'brake 4 marmot'. During check in, I met Krista, who was the site environmental supervisor. She explained that a marmot was a little fury animal similar to a weasel, and they were endangered, with a few of them living around the jobsite. She asked if the 500-gallon fuel tank we sent was a double lined tank. I told her that in the States, we were required to have the tank in an enclosure capable of holding all of the tank's contents if there was a leak. She said that a different tank, meeting Canada regulation would need to be used. We did a barge section inspection, where I explained what and how the various pieces would be assembled. She was quite upset with the 4 spuds, because they had frozen zebra mussels on them and should not have been allowed in the country. I agreed with her, that we had overlooked it, and they would be cleaned prior to assembly.

After cleaning the spuds, we had a meeting to discuss assembly. Because this was a union job, we would have operators to run the crane, ironworkers to assemble, teamsters to transport necessary rigging, and laborers to load and unload necessary rigging. I soon learned that with this many links in the chain, it was going to take a while to assemble. If any of the trades was busy on other tasks on the project, we just stood by.

After about ten days, the barge was assembled and one of the ironworkers remarked that he thought it went well. He asked how long it normally took us to assemble, and I answered that we had a crew of 4 and it would take us 4 days. The barge was assembled upstream of the dam and across the river from where the excavation was to finally take. We were ready to move and they unloaded what they called a tug, which were usually used to raft logs. If the tugs could not handle the current, we would crash into the dam. I picked up the spuds and off we went. With the grace of God, we made it across the river.

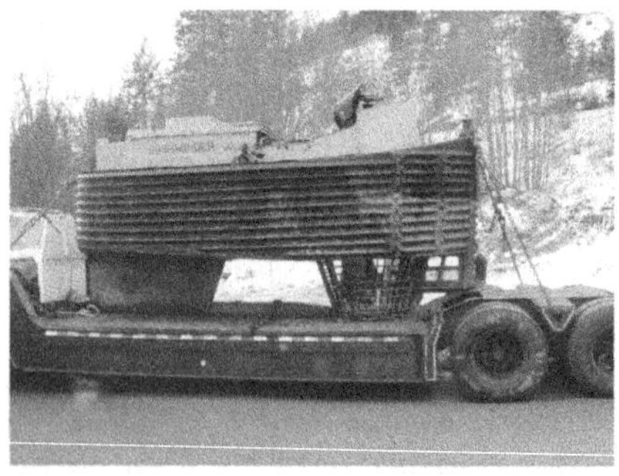

The next order of business was to drill and blast out the rock plug separating the river from the new intake tunnel. The first blast killed a lot of small fish, so they had to modify their blasting methods: Circle the blast area with a 3-inch air hose with small holes, set off a small charge to scare out the fish, then turn on the air compressors to create an air curtain to keep the fish out, and then blast. It still killed fish, but they tried, and we moved on.

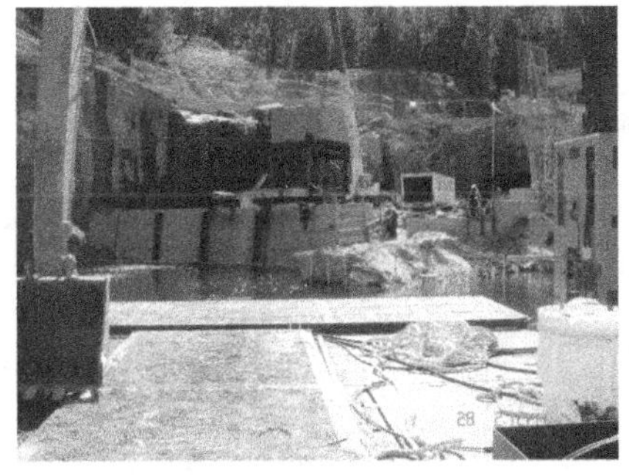

After blasting, we moved the barge in position and moved the blasted rock out into the river, which was very deep. We had a crew of 3 teamsters to operate the tugs, which we did not use, and the excavator operator, Wayne. To move the barge, we had to lower the barge to the water, push back with the excavator, and jack up out of the water. I asked Wayne who operated the hydraulics to raise and lower the barge, and he told me the operators did that. I explained that it took two people, and he said I could operate one and he the other, while the teamsters stood by.

After a few months, the excavation was completed and we demob'd the barge back to the States.

A couple of things I observed were that any equipment operating near the river had to have a plastic tarp below it, and a leak watchman. Even small equipment like welding machines had a plastic diaper below it. Below the dam, at the turbine end, another company was removing the downstream rocks. They were later shut down for a week because they found a dead sturgeon and needed to wait for the results of an autopsy to determine its cause of death. They were shut down for about a week. I was glad our blasting only killed small fish.

One day, I saw a helicopter flying below the dam and was told they were installing transmission lines from one side of the river to the other. There were a couple of men on the receiving side, up on a pole, and the helicopter would grab the power lines and fly them over to the men on the poles. The helicopter would jerk violently up and down as the cable came off the spool as they crossed the river.

On the rock cliff next to where we were working, some men

were lowered on Bosn's chairs, armed with pry bars. They worked their way down, prying loose rocks from the face, I was told they did that all along the highways to stabilize slopes.

CONTAINER BARGE SALVAGE

In 1984, a container barge went aground on the beach at Jacksonville, Florida, and the vessel sank. A salvage company contracted the crane barge 'Michigan', with a Model 4600 Manitowoc crane, and the tug 'Defiance', which were then located at Green Cove Springs, upriver from Jacksonville, to offload the containers onto another barge, in order for them to salvage the container barge.

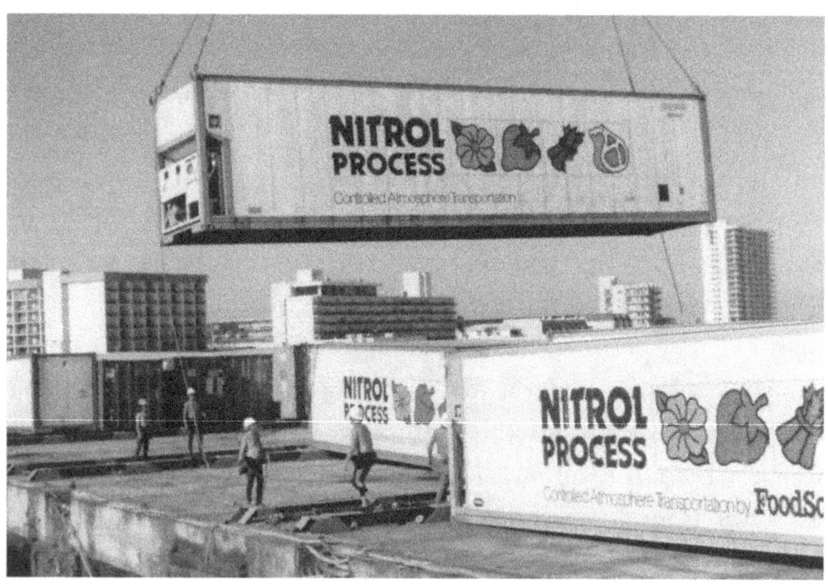

The process was going smoothly, transferring the containers from the sunken barge to the transfer barge. Because we were working near shore in the surf zone, our crane operator, Max Schmike, had to try and time his hoisting of the containers because the crane barge moved up and down. Sometimes his timing was a little off, causing some containers to jerk up folding them.

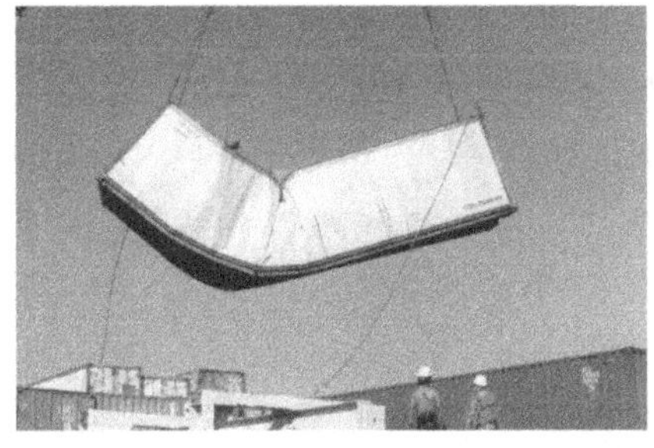

We were working 12-hour shifts, right in front of a Howard Johnson motel where we stayed. We would wade out to the container barge bow, climb a ladder up to the deck, and then cross over to the barge *Michigan*. Early one morning, I looked out my window from the hotel and saw one of our tugs sideways in the surf. It had listed over during the night because the tug had gotten fouled in an anchor cable, disabling it and washing it ashore, before being flooded. The tug *Defiance* tried to help it, but it went in too shallow and hit bottom, shearing both rudders off. Some nights are like that."

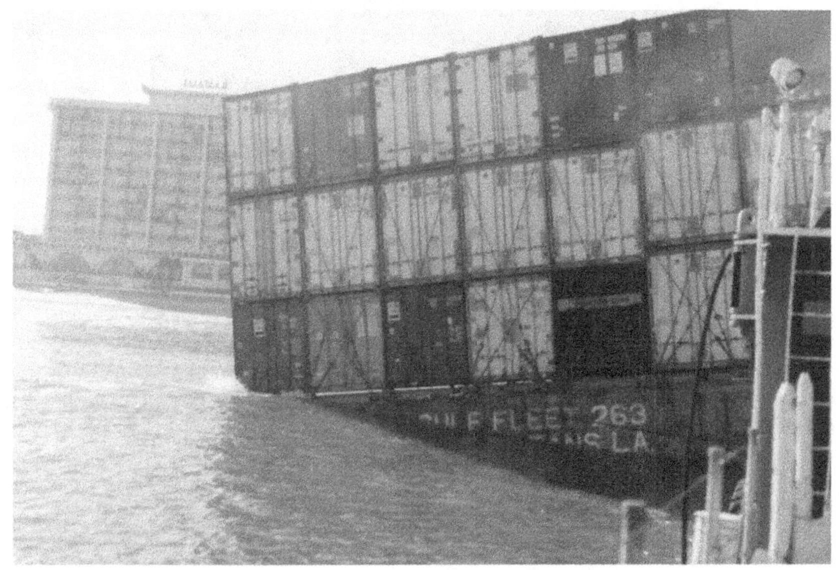

CONRAIL BRIDGE REMOVAL, TOLEDO, OHIO

In 1987, we had a contract to remove an abandoned railroad bridge in Toledo, Ohio. One of the methods used to remove such structures is to use shape charges to blast the steel structure into smaller pieces. Those pieces fall into the river, where they are then removed by a crane. Each span was too heavy for our crane to remove, so we decided to cut them in half, lengthwise, adding falsework to support the remaining half span. We used our barge 'Michigan' with a Manitowoc 4600, 300-ton crane. The barge also had power-down spuds to give us a stable platform to work from.

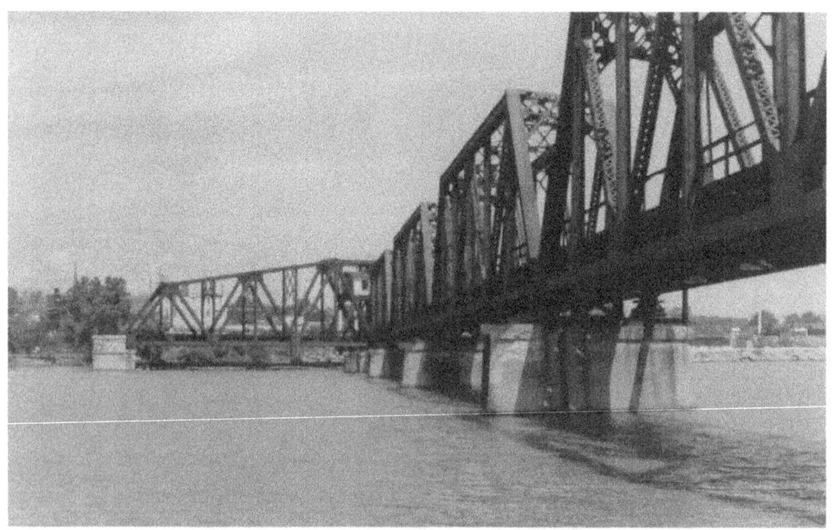

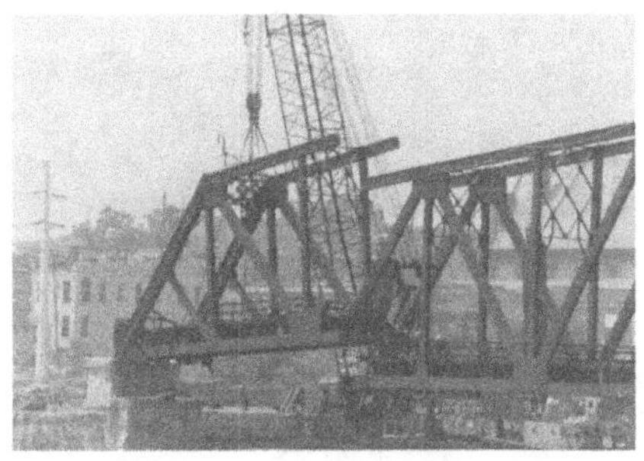

As we began removing the rails and ties, I was approached by the local historical society, telling me that it was historical and needed to be saved. I referred them to Conrail, who informed them that they were fulfilling their permit to remove it because it was no longer needed.

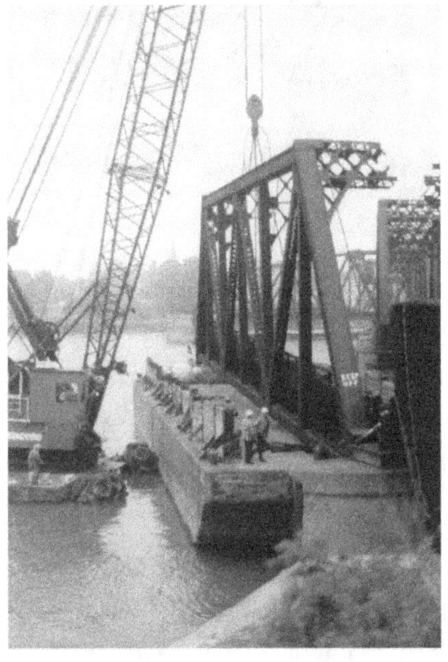

On another day, a city employee arrived at our job trailer to tell me that I needed a plan to remove and relocate the pigeons living in the bridge. I told the employee that the birds were very good at finding new homes on their own.

The last visitors were business agents from a local union who wanted to know how many of their members I would need. I said none, and told them that we were going to use a small crew to pick half spans vs. a larger crew needed to blast and remove the spans from the river. They didn't believe me and set up picket lines that lasted until we removed the first half span, and then they left.

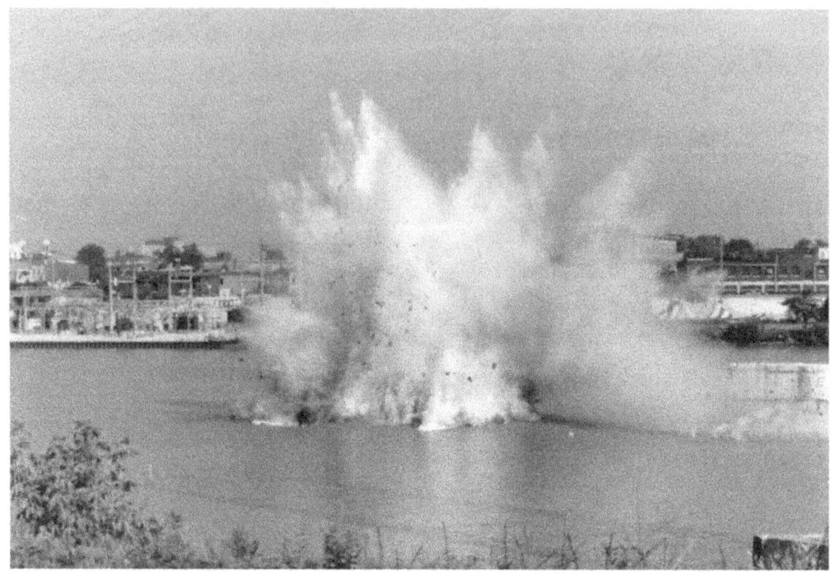

To remove the center swing span, we cut it into smaller pieces before removing them. The last piece was the center piece. The concrete support piers were drilled and blasted then excavated using the crane equipped as a clamshell excavator. The broken concrete was offloaded at the nearby Acme power plant and used for shore protection.

Bob Ojala's Experience Trying to Satisfy Union Officers

I was running a salvage operation for a sunken tugboat at the Port of Indiana, and I was representing the insurance underwriter's claims department. I had recommended that we hire Andrie Inc. for use of their large crane barge in order to raise the tug to the surface. Then we could just pump out the tug. As soon as Andrie's crew arrived, the Union officers showed up. They said that only Union workers were allowed on the property (though Andrie's guys never left the barge). I asked them if they had anyone able to operate the Lima crane and the spud winches, and they said no. However, I needed to hire one Union worker for each Andrie worker on the job, and those union men just sat on the deck of the barge and smoked cigarettes. When I got the invoice from the Port of Indiana, it included huge hourly charges for a Walking Boss and a Straw Boss. I called their business office to have them explain those charges, and they told me those men were observing the operation from their truck on the dock. Most likely, they never left their office downtown!

If you've enjoyed Denny Kempen's stories, take a look at the Appendix at the end of the book, for stories about the following:

- Changes he's seen in construction procedures and equipment, particularly electronics
- Toledo, Ohio, Conrail Bridge removal
- Bethlehem Steel water intake crib installation
- Flint Michigan water intake pipe from Lake Huron (consultant job)
- Mississippi River, shoal removal, maintenance dredging for the Army Corps of Engineers

25

LEONARD ZAUG

My marine life started on the Great Lakes, a place very near and dear to me. I do, however, think what led up to this life on the Great Lakes is very relevant, and that everyone reading this will feel the same way.

I was born on a farm in eastern South Dakota, it's a place I still enjoy visiting often. The world comes to a stop when I'm at the farm. That's one of the better feelings a person can get in the world we currently live in.

Even so, I left the farm and joined the military. I was in the military for four years. I always said going into the military was the best mistake of my life because I grew up very fast during my time serving in the military. I didn't really have a choice. Fortunately, I did make a few good choices, when it was necessary. I completed my military career in Sault Ste. Marie, MI, and decided to stay there and go to LSSU.

The Sault gave me great exposure to Lake Superior, and the Saint Mary's River. Before I got out of the military, I decided to take a test to see what I might be best suited for in life, since I did not know what I wanted to do next. The results surprised me. It indicated that I should either be a supervisor or a writer, even though the same test said my spelling was poor. Anyway, I had no desire to do either one, and I did not feel qualified to do either.

I did go to college part time for a few years before joining the military, but did not finish. That's something I regret to this day. Because I did not have my degree, my life needed to start another chapter, and I knew it. The marine life looked very appealing to me; good money and a very interesting job; what more could you ask for? Because of my prior work experience with farming and the military, I was not sure I had the right background for marine construction, but I got to know several people working in the marine construction business, and the more stories I heard about marine construction, the more I wanted to give it a try.

My first job working marine construction started with LaCross Derdging in Muskegon, MI, in 1978. I was somewhat lost for the first year of my career.

In 1993, I was working for Andrie Inc. We did an interesting job on the Mississippi River that entailed rebuilding a portion of the levee system after it had been breached. The devastation was beyond my imagination; homes were washed away, buildings were half full of mud, all beyond my belief. I saw some of the barges that broke loose out into farmers' flooded fields, with nothing else around them. It made me wonder what it looked like on day-one of the flood. I gained a lot of respect for Mother Nature on that job. My thoughts were that more people in the marine business should witness this level of devastation. There was a lot to learn from the power of one river system.

Andrie was successful in obtaining one of the numerous contracts that were awarded to rebuild the levee system along many miles of the Mississippi River. The project was very high priority, and many stops were pulled. There were very few limitations put on that project. The Corps of Engineers wanted it completed as quickly as possible, and I was put in charge of one hydraulic dredge that was used to rebuild a portion of the levee system that had failed. When that portion of the levee was completed, we just moved to another section and went back to work. Portions of the levee were completely gone, with not even a remnant remaining. I was equipped with one hydraulic dredge, pipeline, two dozers, a tug boat, and a crew.

To be honest, I had only heard of people building a levee; that is, how they did it and the challenges they faced. So I was very grateful I was paying attention that day. The crew was very helpful and offered good advice.

There was no designated place to dredge the sand from. Wherever you could find good sand, it was dredged up and put back on the levee. We could dredge as deep as we wanted and wherever we wanted, the only stipulation being to make the levee out of good material, so that's what we did. There was an onsite representative from the Corps of Engineers working with me. He looked over my shoulders on a daily basis. On occasion, the office crew from the Corps of Engineers would drop by and do an inspection of the levee we had built. We never once heard a complaint.

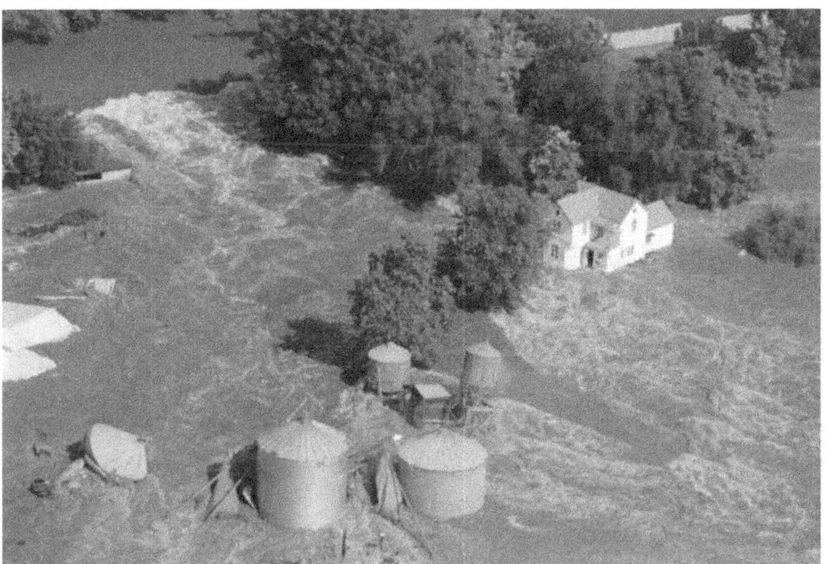

Photo taken of the levee that breeched was taken by Accura Weather

The levees were originally constructed by the federal government. Inspections and maintenance were made by personnel from the U.S. Army Corps of Engineers and designated local groups. The Mississippi River and tributaries' levees currently protect more than 4-Million citizens and 33,000 farms from destructive floods. The levee system was a huge engineering feat.

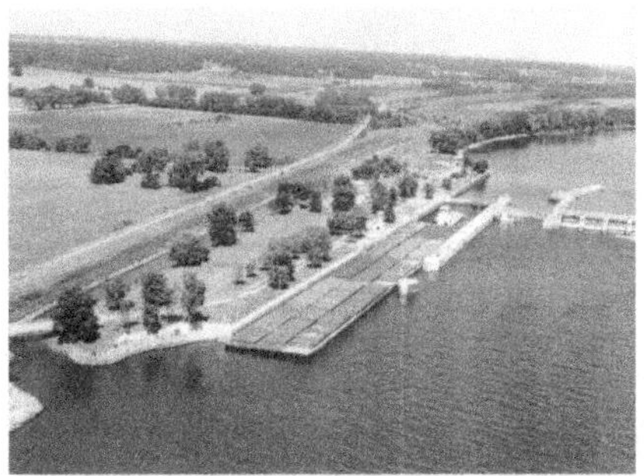

Many people would argue that it causes more problems than it solves. But I believe that if the system is removed, there would be many more catastrophic problems occurring more frequently. Individuals along the Mississippi River would then welcome back the lock and dam and levee system.

26

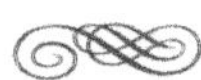

PHIL PETERSON

<u>DELIVERY CAPTAIN – GREAT LAKES AND BEYOND</u>

I have known Phil Peterson for over twenty years. Phil is also a Marine Surveyor, specializing in yachts. However, I met Phil at a Marine Surveyor Seminar and was impressed by his maritime knowledge, far beyond what the average yacht surveyor typically knows. I occasionally asked Phil to fill in for me on jobs when I was not able to attend, and I respected both his knowledge and honesty. I also lean on Phil's expertise when I need to determine valuations for yachts and other small vessels.

Phil had a 100-ton captain's license, which he used for making small-vessel deliveries on the Great Lakes and some out through the seaway. Then Phil started working full time in the "Louisiana Oil Patch," and he was able to upgrade to a Master 1600 GRT license, and had the necessary classes to have the 3000 GT, and Oceans endorsement, sailing oilfield vessels in both the Gulf of Mexico and across the Atlantic to West Africa.

Phil started gaining his maritime experience very early in life, learning to sail on his cousin's 16-foot sailboat on Gull Lake, near Brainerd, MN. But then in 1962, Phil sailed with his Norwegian Great Aunt, eastbound on a trans-Atlantic crossing aboard the SS Stavangerfjord as a passenger, from NYC to Kristinsand, Copenhagen, and finally to Oslo, Norway, to spend the winter with his Norwegian relatives. Phil said The SS Stavangerfjord was scrapped the next year. The following year, he returned, westbound as a trans-Atlantic passenger on the SS United States, crossing from Bremerhaven, to Dover, to LeHavre, and then finally to New York. The SS United States held the speed record for both eastbound and westbound trans-Atlantic crossings.

I guess these experiences whetted Phil's appetite for sailing, because in 1972, Phil departed from San Diego on a Kettenberg 50 sailboat, crewing for an acquaintance from college. Phil's friend took his boat and went back home from Mazatlán, but Phil continued on, finding other boats to crew on. The second boat was a 135-foot converted minesweeper, a near sistership to John Wayne's Wild Goose. Phil saw John Wayne boarding his boat while there. That boat got as far at Manzanillo, Mexico, before stopping, and Phil then caught a bus down to Acapulco, where he signed on a Columbia 40 sailboat with a couple from California. He continued sailing down the coast, and spent a month in Puntarenas, Costa Rica.

Phil taught himself celestial navigation when cruising down the coast, and that knowledge was put to the test when they jumped off for the Galapagos. He spent a month in the Galapagos, and while there, he changed boats to a 61-foot ketch, with a 30-day passage to the Marquesas, Tuamotus, and then Tahiti. He had been on sailboats for about 8 months at that point, and it was time for a change. So, Phil started going over to the commercial dock in Papeete whenever a new vessel came in to see if he could sign on and work his passage to a new location. He just about had a passage on a freighter to Australia, and was told he could join them if he got his gear over there before the pilot came. Just as Phil was leaving, the pilot arrived, so he was unable to go. Then an 1800-ton Finnish refrigerated freighter, the 'Herro', arrived for bunkering, and they were on a trip from the New Hebrides to Italy with a load of frozen fish. Phil was able to sign on with them and made passage to Puerto Rico, a US possession, where he was able to get off and fly home.

In 1973, Phil was selling real estate in the western Twin Cities area and was looking for a way to continue sailing. He talked to Jack Culley, owner of Sailboats, Inc., who was going to sail the company C&C 30 in the Trans-Superior sailboat race that summer. Phil spent weekends sailing on Lake Pepin, and then did the Trans Superior race in late July. That fall, he left real estate and began selling sailboats for Sailboats, Inc.

In 1975, their company boat was 'Andalé', a 1975 C&C 33. They sailed 2,500 miles in 5 weeks: 1) delivering the boat from Bayfield, WI to Port Huron, 2) racing the "Super Mac" sailboat race from Port Huron, up through the Straits , and down to Chicago, 3) doing the Chicago – Mackinac race, then 4) going back up the St. Mary's River to the Soo, and doing the Trans-Superior sailboat race to Duluth. Phil continued with that company, making many sea trials when commissioning new boats, local sailboat races, etc.

In 1979, Phil started spending winters working as a yacht captain on the Stubborn Englishman, a Hinckley Bermuda 40. He spent the first winter in the Bahamas, and other years he also went down to the Virgin Islands, as well as Jamaica and the Cayman Islands. They generally trucked the boat from the Great Lakes, but on one occasion, Phil delivered the boat on its bottom from Bayfield to the Hinckley Company in Southwest Harbor, Maine, when the owner traded it in on a Hinckley 42. Another time, Phil delivered the boat on its bottom to Naples, FL. Both trips went off the Lakes to Buffalo, NY, then across the NY Barge Canal to the Hudson, and down the Hudson to New York City. There they either turned left and went to Maine, or turned right and went to Florida.

In the spring of 1981, Phil sat for his first USCG license, and then ran excursion boats out of Bayfield. In 1982, Phil was given a three-page questionnaire by a regional marine insurance agency, given a list of boats, and was asked to inspect several of them. It was a good gig, but Phil said it seemed like there should have been more to it than that. So, in January

1985, he attended the National Association of Marine Surveyors' annual conference in Florida, and those guys introduced him to ABYC and NFPA. It was a very useful trip.

In 1984, Phil's first delivery was bringing a Swan 40 from Sturgeon Bay, WI, on Lake Michigan, through the Straits of Mackinaw, up the St. Mary's River, and then onto Lake Superior and nearly the length of Lake Superior to Bayfield, WI. In 1984, he also delivered the 'Garhow', a car ferry. The Madeline Island Ferry Line had sold that vessel, and it went down to Chicago. Phil continued to do captain work, and with his salt-water time, he was able to bump his license to a 100 Ton Ocean Operator, so that allowed him to take vessels up to 200 miles offshore.

While working as the Operations Manager at Port Superior Marine, Bayfield, Wisconsin, Phil also did winter captain work on a 50-foot sail-boat operating out of Ocean Reef Marine, in Key Largo. They made trips down the Keys to Bimini, and also a trans-Atlantic crossing from the Canary Islands to Barbados.

In March 1999, Phil was eligible to join the National Association of Marine Surveyors (NAMS) once marine survey work became his primary occupation. He passed the required exam and became a Certified Marine Surveyor. That fall, he was asked to join a delivery crew bringing a 120' car ferry from Lake Champlain to Toledo, Ohio. The vessel had just been purchased by the Madeline Island Ferry, and had a 42' beam, and the controlling width of the NY Barge Canal was 43'. He brought the boat from Toledo to La Pointe, Wisconsin, in early 2000.

Here is a chronological list of Phil's oil patch experience:

2008: When I turned 60, I figured it was time to get my financial house in order. With the blessing of my wife, I packed my seabag and paperwork and headed down to find work in the oilfield. I knocked on a number of doors and ended up getting on as 3rd captain (a mate, really) on a Candy Fleet, 135-foot crewboat out of Morgan City. Times were dicey then, in an economic downturn, and I was laid off about 7 months later. But I had my foot in the door and began taking classes to upgrade my license. I worked on and off for several more crewboat companies, including another stint with the Candy Fleet. I was finally laid off in November.

In **2010**, I took a number of required classes and studied for my 500-Ton Master's ticket. I passed the test in Toledo, OH, on Valentine's Day.

In **2011**, my new license arrived, and I packed my bags and headed back down to Louisiana, and started knocking on doors again. I tried a number of companies and was on first-name basis with some of them. Then I stopped by Gulf Offshore Logistics. The receptionist asked what license I had (500-Ton) and if I had a GMDSS (special radio) license. When I was able to give her the right answers, I was sent in to see the HR Manager. They were sending two crewboats over to Ghana, West Africa, and they were looking for another captain. I said "yes" (after I had talked to my wife), and he said they would be crewing up in about a month. "I'll give you a call." And amazingly, he did. I was in his office the following morning and was sent to DP (Dynamic Positioning) school.

Dynamic Positioning. The control of the vessel is by computer, and initially, the vessel's position is taken from GPS signals. As the vessel approaches the drillship, a cyscan unit is used, which is similar to radar. The cyscan unit on the vessel sends out a signal, which is reflected back from a reflector on the drillship, which is more accurate than GPS signals. There are two levels of DP. DP I has only a single DP system aboard. DP II, aka DP Unlimited, has a redundant backup system aboard in the event the primary system fails. Drillships require supply vessels to have DP II.

We got the boat ready for the trip, but the boat was new, and the Certificate of Documentation hadn't yet come through. So, we departed for Puerto Rico, a US possession, and waited there another week before departing for Ghana.

While in Africa, we also went to ports in the Ivory Coast, Liberia, and Namibia.

Highlights:

- The crew was Ghanaian. Wonderful people. The captains were all USA
- My first job was as a guard boat for the Ocean Rig 'Olympia', a drill ship. The Ghanaian fishermen went out in large dugout canoes powered by an outboard motor and would cast their gill nets and drift. They liked the lights of the drill ship, which attracted fish, and our job was to keep them away. Saw a lot of humpback whales, and we rescued one that had a fish net wrapped around its neck.
- My second job was with the 'Maersk Deliverer', which is a drilling platform. They were initially in Liberian waters, and we ran out of Takoradi, Ghana. It was a 32-hour run out, and 28-hours back due to the current.
- The 'Maersk Deliverer' then had a contract out of Namibia, and we were contracted to support them. On the trip down, we added 12 NM to our voyage and were able to cross the equator on the Prime Meridian, so we became Emerald Shellbacks, a nice upgrade from being just Shellbacks. We returned to Ghana in June of 2012.

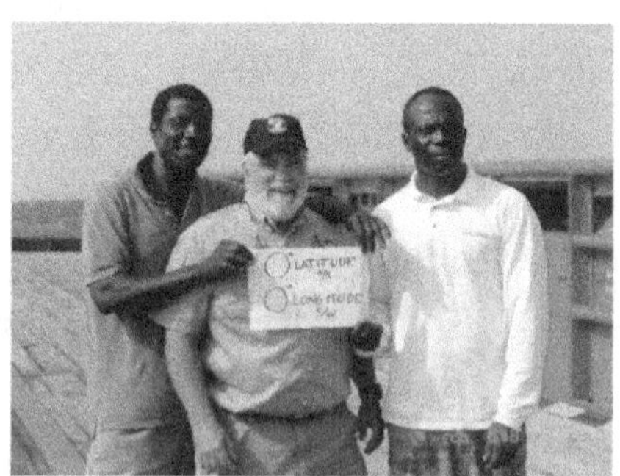

A Shellback is a mariner who has sailed cross the equator. An Emerald Shellback is a sailor who has sailed across the equator at the Prime

Meridian, at 0° N/S, 0° E/W. This is the point where the Northern Hemisphere meets the Southern Hemisphere, and the Eastern Hemisphere meets the Western Hemisphere.

- While in Ghana, my mom was turning 100 years old. It was in the middle of my 8-week hitch. Another captain agreed to return a week early, and the other stayed on an extra week, so I could fly home for the event during the middle of my hitch. I expected my paycheck to show a deduction for the airfare as well as for the time off the boat. But Gulf Offshore Logics took good care of their people, and they kept me on the payroll while I was home, and they did not deduct the airfare. Wonderful company!
- We returned from Namibia to Ghana and picked up a few jobs, but then we were told to return to the States. Just after we left, another job came up, but it was only for 6 months, so we did not return to Ghana.
- The vessel I was on, had dual tonnage. That means that it was about 99 Gross Registered Tons which is a US measurement, and it was also 370 Gross Tons in International Tonnage measurement. To upgrade my license from 500 GRT to 1600 GRT, I had to have time on vessels over 100 tons. And the USCG would accept GRT or GT (ITC) tonnage. So, I was able to upgrade to a Master 1600 GRT license and also had the necessary classes to also have the 3000 GT endorsement.
- Once back in the Gulf of Mexico, I started working on Offshore Supply Vessels (OSVs), which require a higher tonnage license. The following year after we returned from Africa, all of GOL's DP II vessels were purchased by Harvey Gulf International Marine. I ended up on several different OSVs, usually for about a year each. The most interesting was working out of Galveston, where we had a 200 NM run pretty much due

south to service the 'Perdido', a floating drill and production platform owned by Shell. We'd usually be out for a week at a time and have our crew changes back in Galveston. But one time, the vessel was still out at 'Perdido', and we were flown out by helicopter for our crew change. That is the only time my TWIC card has ever been in a TWIC card reader.

• Things started going down the toilet in the oil patch in 2015, and the company started cutting back on things like paying for our flights to and from work. Then they started cutting our daily rate, and finally, in Oct., 2016, it was no longer worth going down for oil patch work.

I came back home and continued to do marine survey work in 2016, with occasional deliveries.

27

⸎

Passenger Excursion Boats

Not every 100-ton passenger excursion vessel captain may deserve to be included in the definition of being a Sweetwater Sailor. However, just because they work on vessels that do not tend to leave their home port doesn't mean that some of them don't gain extensive experience, and they certainly have the dedication that equals those who sail the Lakes' cargo vessels. A select few spend the majority of their lives sailing, sometimes seven days a week during the busy tourist season. They might get to go home at night, but spend very little time with their families until the off-season. And based on my experience, putting up with passengers can be more difficult than the physical labor aboard cargo ships.

I have done marine surveys on most of the Chicago-based passenger excursion vessels over the last 30 years. During my short tenure at the Chicago Harbor Lock, while working with the Army Corps of Engineers, I watched the amazing number of lockages made by these operators. I realized that any preconceived idea that operating a small vessel was easier than operating an ore carrier was entirely wrong. During the tourist season, many of the vessels operate approximately 16 hours per day, having to care for as many as 340 passengers on their larger boats on each trip. Some boats make as many as 4 or 5 round trips during their work day.

The crew has to help the passengers during boarding and disembarking, serve them drinks, answer questions, and protect them from injury. Those vessels doing the Lakefront Cruises need to lock through the Chicago Harbor Lock twice on each cruise, with the deckhands handling lines. The captains are navigating in congested waterways the entire day, dodging pleasure boaters, many of whom rented a boat just for the day, with minimal to no training. Then the boat needs to be cleaned between cruises for the next load of passengers.

I'm certainly not going to imply that the life of the ore boat crew is any picnic, because they also work hard and maybe get dirtier. However, I hope the people watching these boats ply the Chicago River, Milwaukee River, Cuyahoga River, the Soo Locks tour boats, and others, will appreciate the dedication of the people running these excursion vessels. They're under even closer scrutiny by the U.S. Coast Guard because they're carrying passengers, so their training and licensing is just as regulated as those for the crews on the cargo ships. Those operating in Chicago are also regulated by the City of Chicago and the Illinois Department of Natural Resources.

WENDELLA

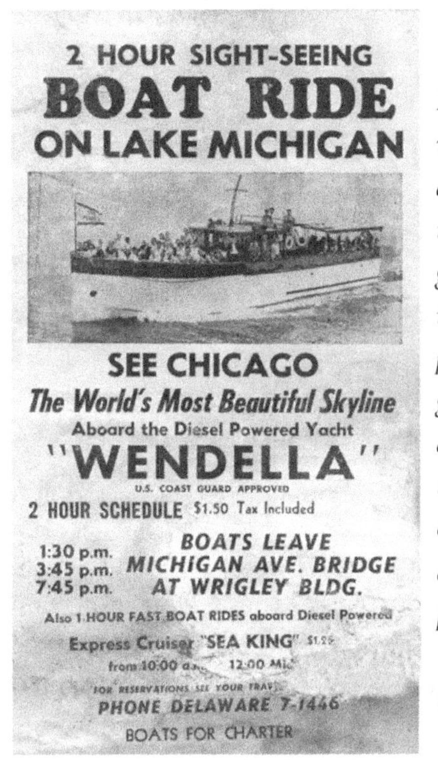

With this said up front, I asked Mike McElroy and Jessica Herum, whom I had worked with at Wendella Sightseeing Company, if they might be allowed to share some background and experiences with me for inclusion in this book. The company's principals, Bob & Mike Borgström, graciously offered to meet with me, along with McElroy and Herum, at their Chicago offices, where we discussed the history of the company, along with numerous anecdotes for possible inclusion in this book.

The following history was related to me by Bob & Mike Borgström:

Before 1935, Bo Albert Borgström worked repairing wooden boats at several shops at Navy Pier (long before it became a tourist attraction). In 1935, he bought a wooden boat that had been damaged in a fire. The boat was named the Wendela (note the single "L"). Albert repaired that boat and started the passenger excursion business.

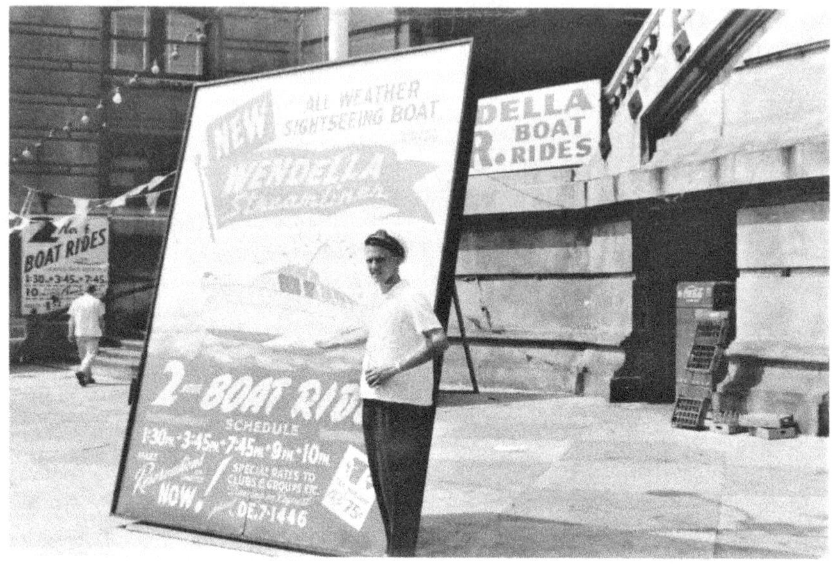

The company actually started as a partnership between Albert Borgström and Art Agra, who was was the grandfather of Bob Agra, the current Vice President/owner of Wendella's competitor, Chicago's First Lady Cruises. When the pair decided to dissolve the partnership, Art set up a competing business on the opposite side of the Chicago River. At times over the years, the competition between the two families became fierce. They both used "Barkers" with large megaphones to attract passengers. However, the Borgströms both said that when personal problems occurred, or safety concerns arose, all of the operators have followed the "Rule of the Sea" to help a fellow seaman in need.

However, this did not mean that some "mean tricks" were not perpetrated by the crew members, such as "stealing their competitors' passengers with trickery. For more weird stories, see below!

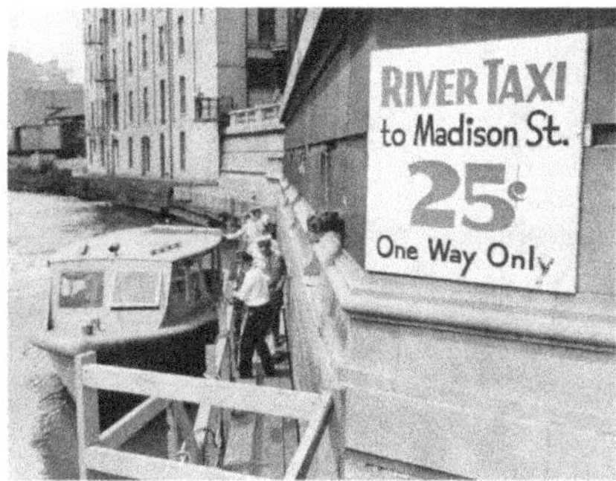

The adjacent photo was taken in 1943 when Wendella briefly operated a River Taxi Service during WW II for sailors from the Great Lakes Naval Training Station, taking them from the CNW train station to downtown.

In addition to the passenger excursion business, Wendella again began to operate their Water Taxi Service in 1962 between various locations on the North, South and Main Branches of the Chicago River. In fact, the Water Taxi can actually make most of these trips faster than the Chicago CTA buses between those locations. In 1963, Wendella and the Chicago North Western Railroad organized a race between the Water Taxi and a Chicago CTA bus from Michigan Avenue to the Madison Street train station, and the Water Taxi beat the bus by ten minutes.

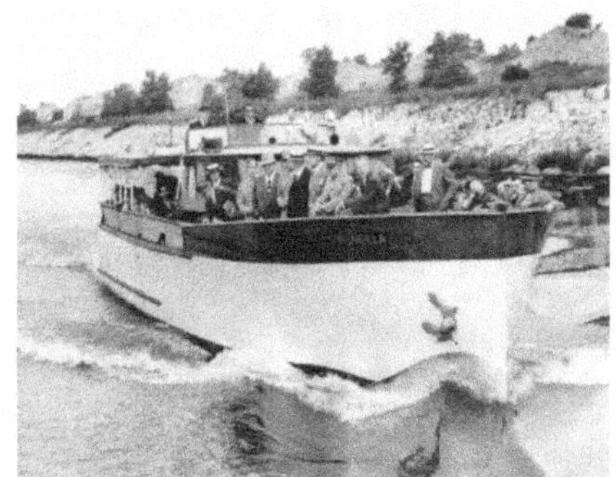

This photo depicts Chicago Aldermen and the newly elected Mayor, Martin Kennelly, taking a Cal-Sag Cruise in 1947, which was a special 6-hour, 70-mile round trip through Chicago's river system, including the Chicago River, Cal-Sag Channel, and the Chicago Sanitary and Ship Canal.

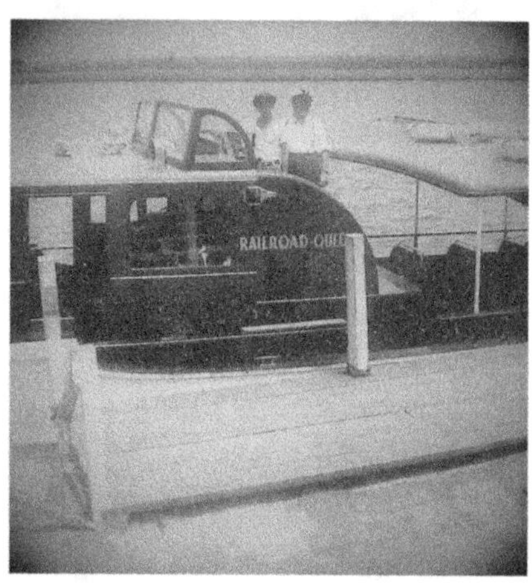

In 1948-49, Wendella operated tours from Navy Pier on the *Railroad Queen* for the Chicago Railroad Fair, which celebrated 100-years of railroad progress.

Wendella and some of their employees have received Commendations from the U.S. Coast Guard for rescues performed on the Chicago River. Because the excursion boats are constantly navigating back and forth, they are many times better situated to respond to someone falling or jumping into the river than the Chicago marine Police.

Weird/Unusual Stories

We discussed numerous serious and funny stories which occurred over the years as follows:

Grounding

One of the unusual stories related by Bob and Mike Borgstrom was about the grounding of one of their excursion tours on the Oak Street Beach. None of the passengers were hurt, and the vessel's captain got them safely ashore. But then the captain left the vessel where it was and walked back to the Wendella docks on the Chicago River. The staff at the dock had wondered why the tour had never returned, and they were shocked to see the captain walking down the stairs to the dock.

Overboard

Another crazy story involved a crew member falling overboard after returning from a fireworks cruise on the 4th of July. Because of the heavy pleasure boat traffic, it was impossible to turn around to retrieve him, so another excursion boat picked him out of the water and dropped him at Navy Pier, where an ambulance took him to the hospital. When the Borgstoms called the hospital to check on his condition, they were told, "He's gone!" They thought the man had died, but it was clarified that he had just walked out of the hospital.

About an hour or so later, that crewmember showed up at the Wendella docks, wearing nothing more than his hospital gown. Not able to find his clothes in his hospital room, he just left and walked back to the dock.

The Helicopter

One of the other excursion companies in town was known for their helicopter, mounted on the upper deck. It was just a shell, with no engine, but it was an "attention getter." The crews at Wendella and Chicago's First Lady joked about having their own helicopter, so one of the crewmembers taped a toy helicopter on top of their pilothouse. Several days later, the toy disappeared, but it ended up on one of the competitor's boats. Despite security guards, it was stolen several more times until it eventually disappeared.

Dead Bodies

As happens in many large cities, bodies are occasionally found in the City's Rivers due to suicides or acts of violence. Therefore, it was not unusual to come to work and find a body floating among the boats along the river. Calling the police would certainly mean giving statements and cause delays in their scheduled tours, so those bodies were sometimes mysteriously moved across the river to the competitor's dock. Enough said.

Loyal Employees

Not all of the employees on these vessels had intentions of becoming a captain, or advancing in their careers. Some were grateful to have a regular job, and some even slept aboard the boats at the end of a long day. The Borgstroms even joked about the fact that if a new employee came to work a bit inebriated, and could fall down the riverfront stairs, but then stand up and go to work, they knew they had found a dedicated deck hand. Those days are over because the Coast Guard frowns on having any crewmember hung over, but in the old days, it was difficult to find crewmembers willing to work 12-14 hour days, 7-days a week, for low pay.

Lots to Learn

During our meeting with Wendella, Mike Borgström mentioned some of the things he learned early on while working with Bob. Bob told Mike that he should never shut down the engines while out on a cruise, and Mike wondered why. Bob then related a story from the old days when one of his captains had taken a cruise out on Lake Michigan with their boat, *Sea King*.

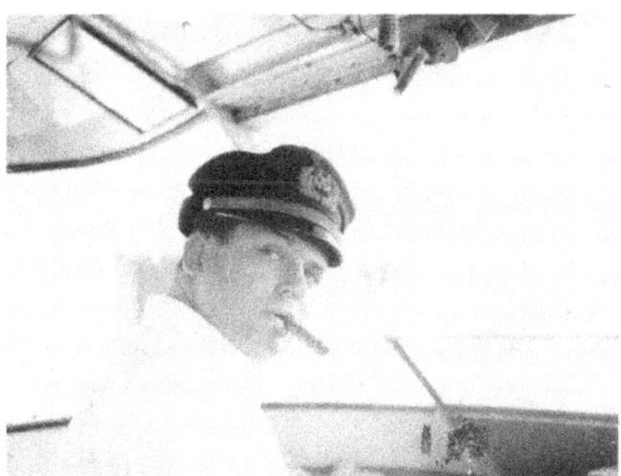

Captain Bob Borgström

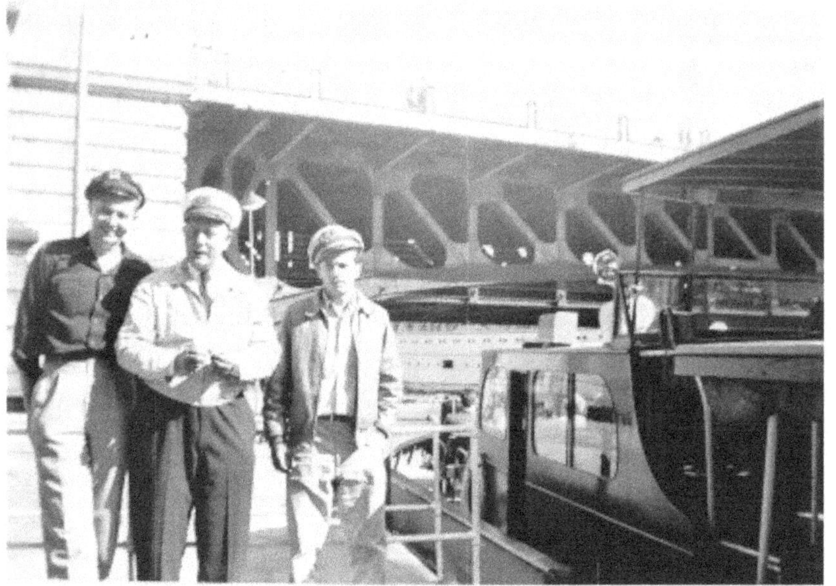

Capt. Bob and crew (Note the cruise ship behind bridge)

The cruise had been chartered by a religious organization wanting to have a memorial service out on the Lake, and they were sitting there with the engines idling. The leader of the passenger group asked the captain if he could please shut down the engine, because the engine noise (an old GM 6-71 diesel) was making it hard to hear. The captain complied.

After the service, it was time to return into the Chicago River, but the captain was unable to start the engine. While sitting out on the Lake, the lights and other electrical equipment had run down the battery. The captain tried to call for help, but there was not enough electrical power to operate the radio. Then the captain tried to use his signal flares, but the flares had apparently become damp and wouldn't ignite.

Because the boat was drifting, the captain thought it would be a good idea to anchor the boat. So, he told the deck hand to throw out the anchor, which he did. However, there was no anchor line attached, so he had literally "thrown out" the anchor.

Back at the Wendella docks, Bob and his father, Albert Borgström, became worried when the boat hadn't returned. When they couldn't contact the *Sea King* by radio, they decided to report the missing boat to the Coast Guard.

A while later, the Coast Guard came into the river with the *Sea King* in tow. The passengers were all wearing lifejackets and were singing religious hymns, such as "Jesus Loves Me...."

From that day forward, the Wendella boat operators have never been allowed to shut down an engine while out on an excursion.

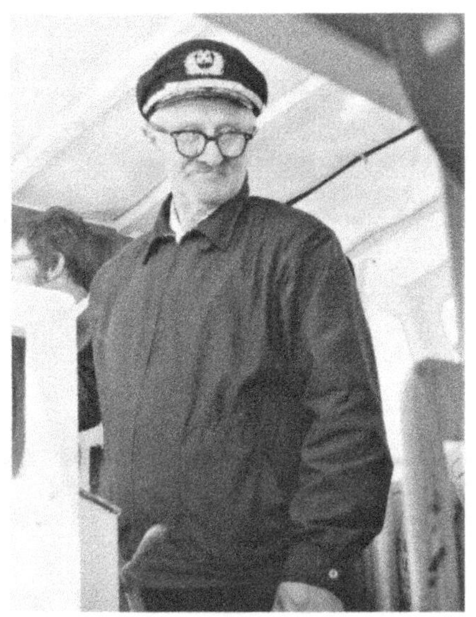

Albert Borgström

The company has owned 22-vessels over the years, with ten of them still in operation. Nine of those vessels were custom-built for Wendella between 1999 and 2022, making it a very modern fleet.

With this history, and their contributions to the Chicago maritime industry, I think you'd agree that the excursion vessel fleets deserve to be included as Sweetwater Sailors!

28

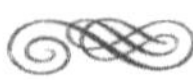

APPENDIX – MORE MARINE CONSTRUCTION STORIES

As promised, here are some of the more technical memories shared by Denny Kempen. Even if you skip over the technical paragraphs, the basic stories are very interesting and well worth reading.

<u>MARINE CONSTRUCTION CHANGES OVER THE YEARS</u>
During my 35 years (close to 40, if you include some consulting work that Bob noted) in marine construction, I saw many advances in the industry. When I started in 1975, dredges and construction projects used wood ranges for alignment, which were usually 4 x 4 plywood targets painted half white, half red, with the back range set higher. When you were 'on line', the targets would appear to be

stacked on top of each other. For night usage, I had to fill kerosene lanterns and hang them on the ranges. Later, these progressed to battery lights, then to laser beams, and finally to GPS. The port and starboard limits were usually plastic, one-gallon buoys. One day while we were dredging the Pte. Mouille disposal channel (near the Lake Erie mouth of the Detroit River), I asked the night time leverman, Art McCoy, how it went during the night? He said, 'Thought I was doing fine until daylight, when a couple of my white buoys flew away.'

When building breakwalls in the early days, ranges and buoys were used to designate limits, and stringlines were set from the top of the rock slope to the bottom of the slope, with a twine strung between them at the desired slope. With the advent of GPS software, someone could set his GPS receiver pole anywhere on the slope and it would give him a slope picture on his screen, showing where he was on the slope, and also the elevation at that point.

Dredging saw a big advancement with the introduction of a cable arm bucket designed by Ray Bergeron. This bucket didn't have any arms from the bowl to the head, because he designed it with chains. This eliminated weight from the bucket. He started designing these for environmental cleanup jobs. His design would close at a level cut, instead of rounded holes, as with conventional buckets. This cut down the amount of over dredging. He also developed a GPS system so that the operator could see the bottom contours in color, designating the amount of material to be removed. If a typical bucket could remove 2-feet per bucket, and there was 6-feet to remove, the colors would change with each bucket until the desired grade was reached, and then the grade color was displayed.

Pipeline laying progressed from divers using bolts and wrenches to pull the pipe joints together to a method developed by Dane Hancock, that used a bulkhead equipped with a hydraulic impeller.

After the divers worked with the crane operator to set the pipe close to the previous pipe, the impeller was engaged, creating equal flow and pressures around the diameter of the pipe. It also drew some water from the previous pipe, creating a vacuum, which drew the two pipes together. Once the pipe was guided to a close position and the hydro-pull started, the pipes were usually joined in less than a minute."

BETHLEHEM STEEL INTAKE CRIB REPAIR

This job is an example of how some projects evolved over time. We were asked to do a dive inspection on the two water intake cribs for Bethlehem Steel, in Portage Indiana. In the spring of that year, a phenomenon known as frazzle ice had occurred to their intake cribs. This occurs when fine ice crystals at the lake surface are drawn to the intake structures and attach to the cribs, sealing them off. Their intakes consisted of a nine-foot diameter pipe at the bottom of the crib, supplying water used by the steel mill.

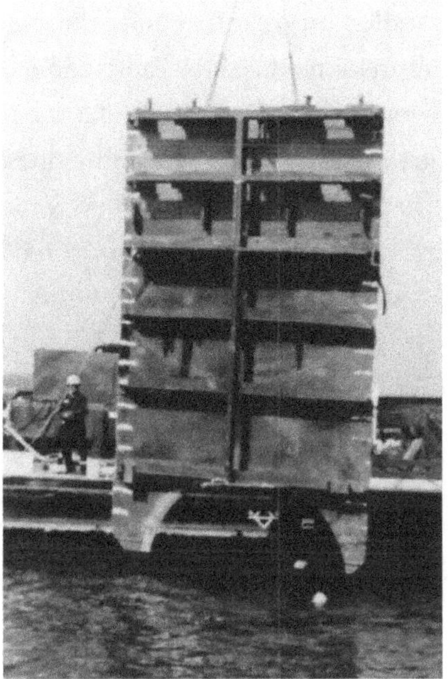

Our dive inspection found that when the ice sealed off the top of the crib, the intake pipe became a suction dredge, it began sucking the bedding stone and sand from beneath the crib, causing the crib to sink a couple of feet. Our divers cut some holes in the steel crib bottom and checked the extent of the voids below the crib. It was decided that the best repair would be to drive steel sheet piling around the crib, and then fabricate a seal piece to go over the intake pipe. After the sheet piling had been installed, we made some toggle-style grout nipples and installed them in the crib floor above the void areas. We then filled the voids with grout pumped from the surface, thus stabilizing the crib.

Another item in this project was to install new intake grates with shear bolts that would shear if they became covered in ice, and swing down allowing water to enter the crib.

The final item was to fabricate an air bubbler ring with air nozzles that we installed on hangers inside the crib. We buried steel pipe from air compressors on shore and connected them to the rings. Flow monitors in the nine-foot intake pipe could trigger the compressors to start if the flow was dropping due to the cribs being restricted by the frazzle ice. The air bubblers would loosen the ice, so it would float away and flow would be restored."

FLINT, MICHIGAN, WATER INTAKE

Most people may be aware of the contaminated drinking water problem in Flint, Michigan, which was a big news story in recent years. Denny acted as a consultant to the company that installed the new, clean water intake from Lake Huron, as he describes below:

In 2014, the owner of Bidco Marine, from Buffalo, New York, called me to see if I would be interested in visiting their jobsite in Lake Huron, north of Port Huron. They were installing a new water intake for Flint, and were having some start-up problems. I had retired the year before, but agreed to meet him at the site and see if I could give him any helpful input.

The project was to dig a trench and lay a subaqueous, 78-inch diameter concrete pipe, and two wood intake cribs. They had hired a barge and tug from Busch Marine, out of Bay City, Michigan, and they loaded the barge with a crane, pipe, and stone for back-fill. They had another barge, equipped with a long reach excavator, to dig the sand trench and side cast the material. Bidco said they had set three pipes but they had settled, so they removed them and reset them during the last week. I spent a couple of days reviewing the excavating and pipelaying operations, and I gave the owner my recommendations. He asked if I would be interested in staying and helping. I said I was retired, but I would stay for a little while.

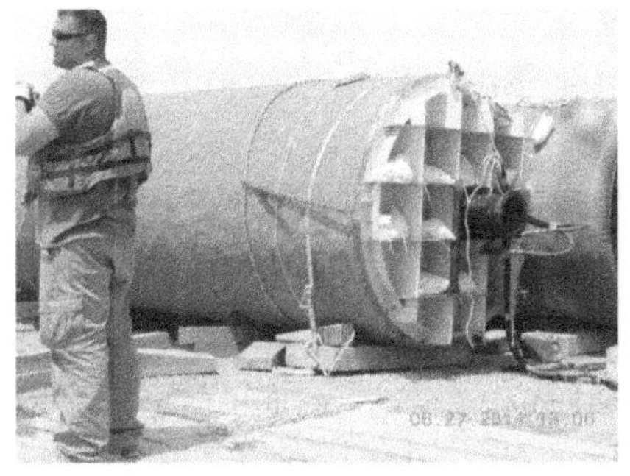

During other pipeline jobs I had worked on, I had been told that one of the keys to laying pipe was the trench being properly excavated. If it's not deep enough, obviously the pipe will not fit, and if it is too deep, it will require more support blocks or stone to support the pipe. Then if it is too narrow, the pipe will run into the side of the trench. We worked with the excavating crew to develop a series of steps to get the trench to proper grade and width.

We also worked on a system of blocks and wedges to support the pipe until it was backfilled. They were using the hydro pull bulkhead, a system developed by Dane Hancock. With his system, the diver maneuvers the pipe he is setting to about 2-3 inches from the previous laid pipe and the hydraulic motor pulls water out of the pipes, centering them, creating an internal vacuum which pulls the pipes together. After checking the elevation of the pipe, it is raised or lowered to the design elevation, and then blocked underneath it until it is backfilled with gravel bedding stone. To steer the pipe, I had them weld a small, usually one-inch-thick steel bar as needed, to either a side or the bottom of the next pipe.

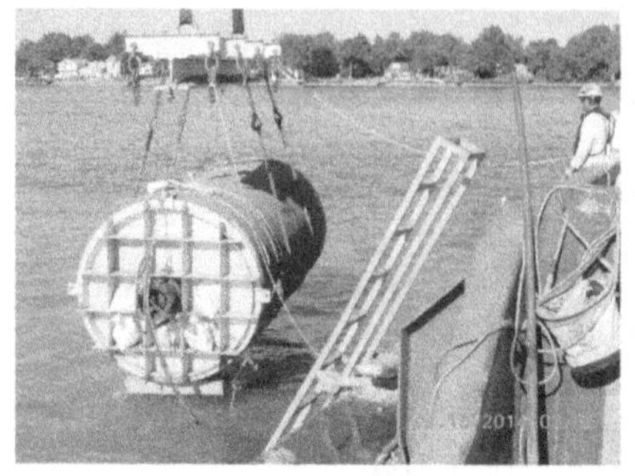

This forced that side or bottom of the pipe to have a slightly wider joint gap, without exceeding recommended design gaps, and this then slightly changed the direction or elevation.

They also had a double-wall, HDPE pipe that was laid on top of the concrete pipe, which would be used to pump chlorine to the intake cribs, killing zebra mussels. The entire pipeline is then backfilled with gravel and sand.

After about a month, they were laying 3 or 4 pipes a day, so I told the owner I was going to leave in a week, because I wasn't adding much more to the procedures for the job. They finished laying the remaining pipes, and the following year they installed the two wooden intake cribs. Other contractors were laying the pipe overland to Flint and ending the water problem in Flint."

I (Bob Ojala) spent my first couple of years as a Naval Architect, working in a small Mississippi River shipyard. I learned to highly respect the talents of these boat operators, and I would visit the Corps of Engineers Lock & Dam operations on the river whenever possible, just to watch them. To help me learn how to design river towboats, my boss at the shipyard arranged a trip for me to ride a Wisconsin Barge Line towboat from Dubuque to Prairie du Chien. Watching a towboat captain perform a "lifting operation" to turn a sharp bend with a string of barges out front is a real experience.

So, here is Denny Kempen's Mississippi River story:

MISSISSIPPI RIVER DREDGING

In 2005, Andrie Inc. was awarded a three-year maintenance dredging contract with the USACE, to remove shoals on the Mississippi and Minnesota rivers, from Minneapolis to south of La Crosse, Wisconsin. The contract required a mechanical dredge with support equipment to be available 24/7, which could be mobilized anywhere on the river to remove shoals that were restricting navigation. As an option to the USACE, a second plant would be available to also remove shoals.

We mobilized our two spud barges, equipped with Model 2400 Lima cranes, two deck barges to transport the dredge spoils to the disposal areas, and two smaller spud barges to move the dozers. In order to get to our reporting area at Winona, Minnesota, from the Great Lakes, we had to cut the tops off our 70-foot spuds because depths on the rivers are usually only 20-30 feet. We also lowered all masts and crane gantries, to allow us getting under that low bridge at Lemont, Illinois, which has a clearance of under 20 feet. When we arrived at the bridge, we added ballast water to the barges to lower them, giving us the required clearance. A river system towing company took our barges from Lemont to Winona. Upon arrival, our crew put the barges and cranes back together.

We purchased two river towboats (I do not understand why they call them towboats when all they do is push). These boats were twin screw and had flanking rudders, making them more maneuverable in close quarters. One of the better decisions we made was to hire three captains that worked on the river system, because they understood the traffic communications, lock procedures, fleeting areas, etc.

One of the boats we bought was named *Sophia Rose*, which we changed to *Rosemary Andrie*. We soon discovered that at about half throttle, it had a terrible vibration. Of course, from what we had experienced with our other boats, we thought it either had a bent shaft, wheel out of balance, or a worn cutlass bearing. Our fleet engineer sent us a man from the Chicago area who had helped him with a vibration problem before. Upon arrival, he set up a series of sensors on the engines and prop shafts, linked to a laptop computer, and we ran the engines at various speeds for about 4 hours. When he left for the day, he said he would analyze the data and give us the answers in the morning.

The next day, the man said the port engine was fine and the problem was with the starboard engine. He said the vibrations were all in the engine, and all of the possible problems that we thought were bad, were actually fine. His findings showed the engine was too high in the front, to high on the right side, to low on the left side, and not properly lined up with the prop shaft. The engine's harmonic balancer was also bad. With his help, we set new engine mounts, installed a new harmonic balancer, and he aligned the engine to the shaft using lasers and his computer. It was unreal, because the boat then ran without any excessive vibrations.

As we operated the boat and passed other boats, they asked if that was the old *Sophia Rose* and did it still vibrate a lot? Apparently, the boat had that problem for a long time. When we said it was the same tug, but we had corrected the vibration, they found it hard to believe.

We were finally sent to our first shoal area with disposal on an island, so, I took our small outboard to the island to check the water depth along the shore to be sure we would know to what draft to load our barge. I was running along the shore when I hit a rock with the prop, knocking a blade off the outboard. When I told our Army Corps inspector what happened, he said that was a rock wingwall, and there were several of them on the river to slow erosion. When I went to the marina for a new prop, they had a 55-gallon barrel full of broken props and a sign that said, 'Deposit wingwall props here'.

We had set up our crane with a computer monitor that would show the operator the area to dredge, with different contour colors. When he removed a bucket, the color would change the remaining material to a different grade color. We also bought two cable-arm buckets that cut a 10-foot x 10-foot square area. These buckets do not have any arms or top piece, but use chains for arms, making them lighter than a conventional bucket. This style was developed by Ray Bergeron from Trenton, Michigan, and built in a shed behind his house. Most contractors have at least one of his buckets, which he builds to their specifications.

The first year was a learning curve, as most jobs are. I was impressed when a river tow would pass us, with usually about six barges, and we had to move just out of the cut. When asked if they had enough room, they would politely say, 'Sure, just don't move,' and some passed by with only 10 feet between us. Their skill was amazing. We also hired a couple of river deckhands, which was necessary when cabling our barges together, moving from site to site. They had worked with the captains and knew how to rig the cables properly between barges.

The material we removed was mostly sand until we got closer to Minneapolis. Then it was a soupy silty sand, which would not stack at all. A lot of the disposal areas had been used for years and contained a lot of sand, which forced us to push the sand uphill, and very high. At one of the disposal areas, I was pushing sand uphill with our D-6 dozer, and about halfway up, the track broke a pin, and it came apart. The mechanic I called asked where it was, and when I told him, he said it could not be repaired there. I finally talked him into trying, and with a lot of elbow grease, and a few choice words, we put it back together. At another site, the dozer engine blew up. The mechanic pulled the axle so it would roll without brakes, and he road it down the hill.

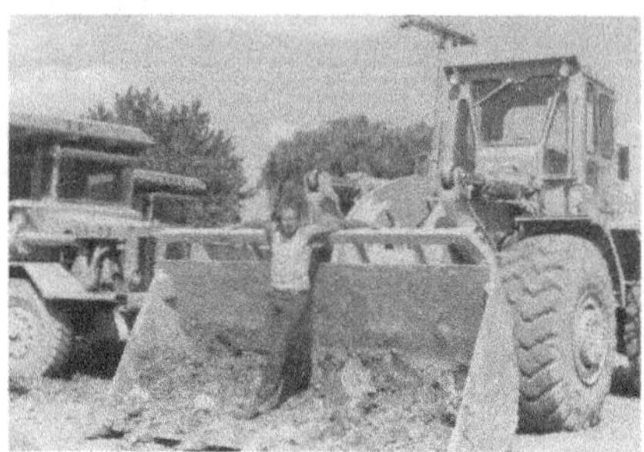

The second year of our contract, they released our second plant, so we used one plant to dredge and the second plant to offload at the disposal sites. Before we started the third year, Andrie decided to sell their marine construction equipment, and we subcontracted the last year to a local contractor."

29

ABOUT THE AUTHOR

Bob Ojala is an author, writing both non-fiction and fiction books, generally dealing with life in the maritime industry. His novels center around real-life events where possible, changing names and locations to protect privacy.

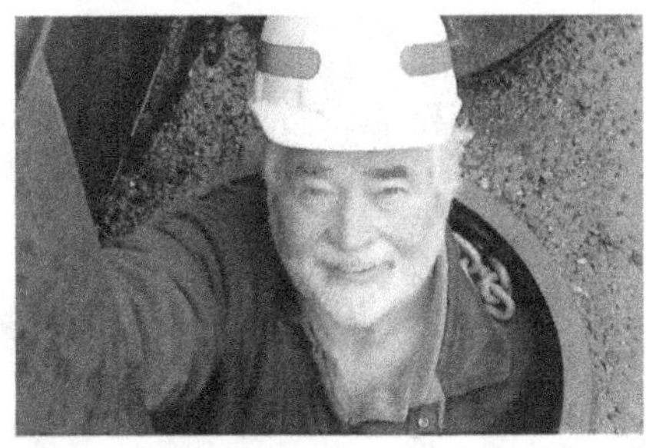

Bob is a Wisconsin native with Finnish roots. His father was a Merchant Mariner for 32 years, giving Bob the interest in the Maritime Industry, but not the desire to be a sailor.

Bob worked as a Naval Architect, designing small passenger vessels, tugs, and barges after graduation. However, Bob found he enjoyed working in the shipyard, with the workers, more than sitting in the design office.

When the opportunity came to join the American Bureau of

Shipping, working as a Field Surveyor, inspecting ships, and equipment going into shipbuilding, Bob thought this was what he was looking for.

Eventually, Bob started his own Marine Surveying & Consulting business. Because Great Lakes clients were slow in changing loyalties, Bob began traveling the world, surveying (inspecting) cruise ships, tankers, drydocks, historic vessels, and even some warships. Bob also performed investigations of accidents, pollution incidents, and several accidental deaths.

Bob always wanted to document his father's career as a sailor on the Great Lakes, which is what motivated him to put together the first Sweetwater Sailors, but he saw it was important to document all of the Great Lakes sailors, not just one segment of the industry. This latest book tries to show "The Rest of the Story" with more women sailors, sailors' families, and the more "unusual" sailors on the Great Lakes.

Bob Ojala's books include:

- Autobiography of a Ship's marine Surveyor - Surveyor's Are Made, Not Born
- World Travels & Adventures of a Ship's Marine Surveyor (Autobiographical)
- Sweetwater Sailors (non-fiction, real-life stories from Great Lakes mariners)
- A Tugboater's Life (Contemporary Romance based upon Great Lakes Marine Construction)
- The Tugboater Family (stand-alone, but flowing characters from A Tugboater's Life)
- Crew's Ship Affairs (Life on a large cruise ship, BELOW the passenger decks)
- KIDNAPPED – A Tugboater's Tale (Human Trafficking in middle-America)

More are on the way, such as Great Lakes Commercial Fishermen